Leading Schools in an Era of Declining Resources

Every day, school leaders across the country have to make difficult decisions in this economically demanding environment. If you are a leader facing this challenge in your own school or district, this is the book you need! Experienced educators Johnston and Williamson offer practical advice to help you tackle a variety of tough issues, including staff reductions and program termination. You'll learn how to . . .

- Wring every bit of performance out of every available dollar
- Plan innovations and evaluate their effectiveness
- Engage faculty and the community
- Streamline operations using digital technology and social media
- Use four strategies—Reduce, Refine, Reprioritize, and Regenerate—to make your school more efficient and effective

Each chapter is filled with tips, tools, exercises, and mini-cases to help you apply these ideas to your own situation. You'll gain the confidence and knowledge to manage your budget while ensuring your students get the full benefit of a quality education.

J. Howard Johnston is Professor of Secondary Education at the University of South Florida. He is the recipient of the NASSP's Distinguished Service Award and NMSA's John Lounsbury Award for lifetime achievement. He is also the author of seven books and more than 150 publications.

Ronald Williamson is Professor of Educational Leadership at Eastern Michigan University. He has served as Executive Director of the National Middle School Association and as President of the National Forum to Accelerate Middle Grades Reform. He is the author of seven books.

Leading Schools in an Era of Declining Resources

By J. Howard Johnston and
Ronald Williamson

Routledge
Taylor & Francis Group

NEW YORK AND LONDON

First published 2014
by Routledge
711 Third Avenue, New York, NY 10017

and by Routledge
2 Park Square, Milton Park, Abingdon, Oxon, OX14 4RN

Routledge is an imprint of the Taylor & Francis Group, an informa business

© 2014 Taylor & Francis

Library of Congress Cataloging-in-Publication Data

Johnston, J. Howard.
Leading schools in an era of declining resources / J. Howard Johnston, Ronald Williamson.
    pages cm. — (Eye on education)
    Includes bibliographical references.
  1. Educational leadership—United States.   2. Education—United
States—Finance.   I. Williamson, Ronald D.   II. Title.
LB2805.J638   2014
371.2—dc23   2013049329

ISBN: 978-0-415-73482-0 (hbk)
ISBN: 978-0-415-73481-3 (pbk)
ISBN: 978-1-315-81970-9 (ebk)

Typeset in Optima
by Apex CoVantage, LLC

This book is dedicated to our families for their patience and understanding of our work schedules and deadlines, and to all of the principals, teachers, district officials and community members who provided us with guidance, examples, and helpful criticism.

Contents

Meet the Authors

J. Howard Johnston is professor of secondary education at the University of South Florida. Previously, he served as a professor of education, dean of education, and dean of the graduate school of education at the University of Cincinnati. He has authored over 150 works on education and has presented more than 2000 invited papers, lectures, and keynote addresses in all 50 U.S. states, across Canada, and in more than a dozen countries in Europe, South America, Asia, and the Caribbean. In addition to numerous books, he has published in virtually all of the major professional and scholarly journals devoted to teaching, learning, and leadership. Howard received his BA and MA from the State University of New York, New Paltz, and his PhD from the University of Wyoming.

Howard is the recipient of the National Association of Secondary School Principals' Distinguished Service Award, the National Middle School Association's (NMSA) Presidential Award for Excellence, the Gruhn-Long Award for lifetime service to middle-level education, and NMSA's John Lounsbury Award for lifetime achievement. He has served on the Board of Trustees of the NMSA and the Council on Middle Level Education for the National Association of Secondary School Principals. In addition to his extensive consulting work with school districts and other educational agencies, he is currently engaged in a unique program to provide personalized professional development for principals in Oregon GEAR UP schools.

Along with co-author Ron Williamson, Howard writes the blog "Doing More with Less: Leading Schools in an Era of Declining Resources," an interactive community of school leaders sharing practical ideas about adjusting to, and even prospering in, the new economic environment, http://leaders-doingmorewithless.blogspot.com.

Ronald Williamson is a professor of educational leadership at Eastern Michigan University. He previously taught at the University of North Carolina at Greensboro and served as a principal and executive director of instruction in Ann Arbor, Michigan, public schools. Ron works with schools and leadership teams throughout the nation on school improvement projects and prepares research briefs for Oregon GEAR UP. He previously served as executive director of the National Middle School Association, as a member of the Middle Level Council of the National Association of Secondary School Principals (NASSP), and as president of the National Forum to Accelerate Middle Grades Reform. He received the Gruhn-Long-Melton Award from NASSP in recognition of his achievement in secondary school leadership, the Teaching Excellence Award from the University of North Carolina at Greensboro, and the Alumni Teaching Excellence Award from Eastern Michigan University.

Ron is the author of articles, chapters, papers, and books. His work has appeared in all the major professional journals serving secondary school teachers and principals. He provided direct service to several large urban districts as a leadership coach in projects funded by the Edna McConnell Clark Foundation and the Galef Institute of Los Angeles. If you would like information about Ron and his work, contact him through his website: http:// ronwilliamson.com.

Preface

American schools have been hit with a tsunami of budget cuts and retrenchments that have buffeted most, crippled some, and devastated others. At the same time, they are faced with demands for ever-increasing accountability for student performance, major curriculum revisions brought about by new state and Common Core standards, and more public scrutiny and criticism for lapses in performance. Educators might lament these changes and rally against them, but they are the current reality in our schools—what U.S. Secretary of Education Arne Duncan and others have called "The New Normal." Quite simply, it's the way things are going to be for a while—maybe a long while—so the challenge for school leaders is pretty much the same one they have always faced: providing the best education possible with the resources available to them. Certainly the resources are fewer, and society's expectations for the "best education possible" is evolving almost daily, but the job is the same; it's the times that have changed.

Leading Schools in an Era of Declining Resources is written for school leaders who must make practical decisions about how to adjust to, and even prosper in, this new economic and demanding environment. Neither of the authors are fiscal experts. In fact, they're not particularly interested in school finance at all. But both Ron and Howard have been in the same position as so many of today's school administrators—having to do more with less, sometimes a lot less, and sometimes quickly and definitively. Both have worked in states that suffered tremendous economic hardship, sometimes while the rest of the nation prospered, and both have faced the awful stress of cutting personnel, consolidating, reducing or eliminating programs, and working with angry staff and anxious parents and students to make their institutions fit new fiscal realities.

This book is more about schools and the people in them than it is about money. It's about how leaders can make the most of what they have, reduce their budgets with courage and compassion, change schools to make them more efficient and more effective, and make sure that students get the full benefit of a quality education, even if it doesn't always look like the one we had ourselves. In short, it's about leadership in the New Normal environment.

The book is written for practicing school leaders, although we hope that it will also be read by school board members and lay people who have a special interest in their community's schools. Frankly, it is *not* a treatise on how unreasonable the budget cuts are for schools or an argument for increased funding—although both authors agree, fundamentally, with both of those positions.

Instead, it starts with an acceptance of the current situation. And, while both the authors and other educators may work toward increased funding and more reasonable performance expectations for schools, those are goals best achieved through political activism and advocacy. It is the school leader's job to make their schools work as well as they possibly can with what they have, and that is what we seek to help them do. That's not to suggest that leaders can't negotiate, horse-trade, or bargain to make budget reductions less problematic for their schools. In fact, the chapters of this book are loaded with tips on how to negotiate some relief and tools for getting the information you need to do so.

Beyond those tips, the chapters contain basic information about school resources, advice on how to wring every bit of performance out of every available dollar, suggestions for actually increasing revenue, and examples, tools, and resources from practicing school leaders who have managed to work effectively in the New Normal environment.

We open the book with a brief tour of the New Normal landscape, some research on how we got here and why the current conditions are going to prevail for a while. Then we get right to work on four major strategies for dealing with the New Normal realities—the Four R's:

- Reduce: how to reduce the budget courageously and compassionately while preserving the core functions of the school.
- Refine: how to improve basic school operations and processes through innovation and the judicious use of technology.

- Reprioritize: how to change the way schools do business to reduce resource consumption and still improve student achievement.
- Regenerate: how to generate new resources and create sustainable operations to ensure the long-term health of the school despite fluctuations in revenue.

We also include a major section on the leadership skills and strategies needed to prosper in this new environment, and a vast array of tools and resources to help school leaders do their incredibly challenging work.

This book can be used in several ways. You can certainly read it straight through, gather as much information as you can, and use the resources to approach budget challenges and issues. You might also use the book as a study resource for your school's leadership team. Increasingly, districts and individual schools are using a professional resource as a springboard for discussion, deliberation, and planning around critical issues, and we tried to ensure that this book has the resources so it can be used that way as well. Finally, this might be a useful resource for board members, community leaders, interested parents, and teacher-leaders who are involved in either making budget decisions or adjusting to them. We avoid technical jargon and most of the intricate details of school financial policy-making, so the book speaks directly to the people who do the work of schooling in America.

And because this is a *New* Normal, there are very few experts (although a lot of opinionated pundits) who have all of the answers. In fact, the one thing that can be inferred from all that has been written about how schools can prosper in this new reality is that there is no silver bullet, no magic wand, and no off-the-shelf program that will solve our problems. Solutions are going to take hard work, thoughtful analysis, creative thinking, and tremendous dedication to providing the best education we can for all of our children. So please join us in sharing your wisdom about how you and your school are prospering in the New Normal environment by linking to our blog: http://leadersdoingmorewithless.blogspot.com/, sponsored by Practical Leadership, LLC.

J. Howard Johnston
St. Petersburg, Florida
Ronald Williamson
Saline, Michigan

Welcome to the New Normal

Part I contains only one chapter, but it may be the most important one of all. It is where we examine—and try to help the reader understand—the origins, effects, and likely outcomes of the New Normal environment in our schools and our nation.

Our research has yielded some very important and inescapable conclusions. First, the New Normal is not just a set of fiscal conditions. Instead, it is the result of a much more complex set of variables that interact to produce fundamental and lasting changes in American life and the role of schools in our society. It represents a convergence of economic, political, technological, demographic, environmental, and global forces that are moving with lightning speed through every aspect of our individual lives and our communities.

All of these forces have taken on a life of their own, and none of them are under the control of the schools or school leaders. Furthermore, they aren't going away. The changes that are occurring now will alter the fabric of our society for generations to come, so there is no point in trying to "wait out" the turmoil of these multiple transitions in the hopes that things will get back to normal—also known as "the way things used to be."

The second conclusion is that school leadership now requires not only managing an enormously complicated enterprise that involves hundreds of employees and thousands of clients, it now demands that leaders help their students, staff, and community understand the New Normal and how it affects their schools. Then comes the hardest part of all: helping everyone adjust to these changes so that our schools remain productive, responsive, and competitive in a global environment.

1 Good News, Bad News

Introducing the Landscape of the New Normal

You never want a serious crisis to go to waste.

Rahm Emanuel

In a speech to the American Enterprise Institute, Secretary of Education Arne Duncan said,

> I am here to talk today about what has been called the New Normal. For the next several years, preschool, K-12, and postsecondary educators are likely to face the challenge of doing more with less. My message is that this challenge can, and should be, embraced as an opportunity to make dramatic improvements. I believe enormous opportunities for improving the productivity of our education system lie ahead if we are smart, innovative, and courageous in rethinking the status quo. It's time to stop treating the problem of educational productivity as a grinding, eat-your-broccoli exercise. It's time to start treating it as an opportunity for innovation and accelerating progress.

The Bad News

In slightly more than 100 words, Duncan described succinctly and clearly the challenges faced by teachers, school leaders, and policy makers: the nation will call upon us to produce better results for more students, in less time, and with fewer resources than at any time since the Great Depression.

And the price for *not* achieving those standards will be very high indeed—loss of teacher pay, termination or reassignment of school administrators, closing of failing schools, retention of non-achieving students, and even state take-over of low-performing districts. Teacher tenure has been under attack in numerous states, and 18 states have modified their tenure systems to make it easier to fire teachers who do not produce high student achievement. Several have actually eliminated tenure for new teachers altogether.

Increasingly, accountability for student learning has been shifted to the teachers and school leaders who manage our nation's learning programs, and any vestiges of immunity from the consequences of poor student performance have been swept away in a tsunami of legislative initiatives, executive orders, and federal programs that reward states that embrace accountability and reduce resources to those that do not.

At the same time, public funding for education is being reduced dramatically in virtually every state in the nation, and even states that maintain level funding or manage small increases usually do with big conditions attached to the new money.

The Good News

Is it really possible to find *any* good news in this avalanche of negative reports and press coverage? Many educators think so.

In his remarks, Secretary Duncan hints at a position that Rahm Emanuel, then chief of staff for President Obama, stated very clearly (2008): "You never want a serious crisis to go to waste. What I mean by that is it's an opportunity to do things that you did not think you could do before." After cataloging a very daunting list of challenges facing the nation, including the loss of education funding and the problems faced by America's schools, Emanuel adds, "The good news . . . the silver lining . . . is that the problems are big enough that they lend themselves to ideas from both parties for the solution."

Although not talking specifically about education, Mr. Emanuel's remarks have special relevance for school people—the problems of funding, productivity, accountability, competition, student attrition, and global competitiveness are now sufficiently big that everyone must begin to think about new ways of doing business more efficiently, effectively, and flexibly. We no longer hear talk of "restoring" funding to make schools the way they were, or of returning to what we once had. The national conversation now is about how to move forward to serve an increasingly more diverse population of young people as they prepare for a more uncertain and competitive global future.

In essence, for the first time in decades, school leaders have been given permission—indeed are being compelled—to think about ending some of the things that schools have always done, taking on new obligations and responsibilities mandated by a new global economic environment, and changing just about everything else. As one superintendent put it in a conversation with Howard Johnston, "I hate the fact that we have less money, but this current [budget] crisis does give us some leverage to do things we've wanted to do . . . needed to do . . . but lacked both the internal and public support, and, frankly, the political will, to do."

The Leadership Challenge

One of the ironies of school leadership preparation programs is that they tend to focus on educational systems (including individual schools) as they are, rather than as they could be or probably will be. For the most part, experienced school administrators and leaders who are familiar with research in the field teach aspiring and fledgling school leaders how to do the complex job of educational administration. Programs are prized for being practical, down to earth, and connected to the realities of contemporary school life. Internships and apprenticeships pair leaders-in-training with practicing school administrators so they can learn the subtle demands of daily operations and the unwritten, but essential, rules of successful leadership.

Only rarely are these aspiring leaders confronted with some of the huge forces swirling around the school—economic, demographic, or technological—that shape much of what happens inside the school. Even more rarely are they asked to analyze these dynamic forces and think about how they may be called upon to modify their leadership to meet the challenges they present.

As a result, most novice school leaders are prepared for a smooth move into an existing school and for practicing the craft of leadership in ways that are remarkably similar to those of their peers in neighboring schools—or even in ways that resemble the leader they replaced. Indeed, when external forces produce a profound effect on the school, the response is usually to treat it as a problem to be solved so that "we can get back to normal" as soon as possible. Leaders are rewarded by their staff, and often by their district, when they keep things on an even keel and not make too many changes in the school, no matter how desperately the school may need to change.

But that was before the rapid evolution of the New Normal. Now, as Rahm Emanuel points out, we have hit a period of crisis: funding has been slashed in most states, community demographics are changing, the demands placed on schools are accelerating, and growing competition from alternative forms of schooling have sprung up all over the nation. Charter schools, alternative schools, virtual schools, home-schooling, private schools, specialty schools, and partnership schools with businesses or universities have increased competition for a dwindling pool of students and a shrinking bank of public resources.

Embracing the Crisis

So what are leaders to do to make certain that their schools don't "waste" this crisis, but use it as an opportunity to make necessary, sustainable changes that prepare the children in their communities to prosper in the 21st century? How can school leaders sustain their own optimism about the future of their schools, and convey that optimism to their staff, students, and communities, so that they create a climate of growth and development rather than entropy and decline?

> I have not failed. I've just found 10,000 ways that won't work.
>
> Thomas A. Edison

Fortunately, there are many lessons to be learned from private sector businesses, government agencies, and other schools that have responded, even embraced, the challenges presented by the New Normal. The cyclical nature of business has driven many private sector leaders to learn to do things very differently—and learn it quickly. Funding cuts to public institutions other than schools, such as libraries, transportation systems, social services, and public health and safety agencies, have forced leaders in those fields to create lean, streamlined systems for fulfilling their goals and to use technology to attain new levels of efficiency. Other school and school district leaders who are ahead of the curve on adjusting to funding cuts because of regional economic variations have also learned how to deliver high-quality educational services, sometimes even better than the ones that existed during periods of full funding, at a lower cost and with greater effectiveness in serving a diverse population.

These approaches are not always easy, and many are not always embraced with enthusiasm initially by staff, parents, or even students. But as educators' responses to the New Normal evolve and mature, many of these approaches have established a successful track record and have been accepted, and even celebrated, by the same people who initially resisted them.

The Four *R*'s

The strategies and approaches for leading in a New Normal world that we explore in this book fit into four categories: *Reduce*, *Refine*, *Reprioritize*, and *Regenerate*—the Four *R*'s for leading schools in an era of increasing demands and declining resources. The effective implementation of these strategies depends on a leader's deep commitment to creating *sustainability* in the school community, accomplished practice of a full repertoire of *leadership skills*, and a *climate* of inclusiveness and deliberation that encourages open debate and consensus-building.

Reduce means making necessary cuts in a fair, reasonable, transparent, and humane manner. Budget cuts have called for commensurate reductions in many aspects of school operations—from transportation to basic curriculum options—and school leaders are called up on to exhibit both courage and compassion in making these difficult choices. Often these choices come down to continuing to support something that, traditionally, has been a strong part of the school curriculum or eliminating this very satisfying program in order to divert resources to more contemporary demands. And often it requires new levels of creativity and bold action on the part of school leaders.

An Ohio principal faced with declining enrollments had to reduce her school's staff by three members—a physical education teacher who was retiring, a recently hired science teacher, and the school's computer network manager, who left the school for more lucrative employment in a local hospital. At the same time, the district was pressing forward with a computer-based, individualized instructional program that allowed the burgeoning English Language Learner (ELL) population to keep up with their English-speaking classmates in core subjects.

The principal approached the young science teacher and asked if he would be willing to give up his tenure-earning teaching position if she could arrange for him to be appointed to the network management slot. He agreed, and she pitched a plan to the superintendent: her school would share part of the network manager's costs if the district and one other school could pick up a share as well. When that was settled, she then asked the continuing education department at a local college if they would give the fledgling network manager a slot in their usually expensive network management course. They granted a scholarship to the new network manager, and he attended the training in the evenings after his work at school was finished.

Everyone realized that a certified network manager with a science background was a very marketable individual, but the district bet on the fact that the young man would remain in the school long enough to finish the certification program and get the new ELL program running smoothly.

In this case, the principal acted boldly in several ways: she offered an opportunity for a bright young professional to give up a tenure-earning teaching position in favor of a less-secure staff job; she linked her solution to a district-wide cost-saving initiative that appealed to the superintendent; and she exploited a local educational resource to help the young teacher retrain for the new position and greatly enhance his prospects for employment in the future.

This story has several important outcomes. First, the principal got significant savings by sharing the cost of a person who was vital to the school's operation. Second, she achieved greater efficiencies in staffing because the relatively few students who signed up for the young teacher's science courses could be redistributed to other classes. Third, the science-teacher-turned-network-manager became an integral part of a new initiative in the district that may help secure his future better than tenure would have.

Finally, other staff saw that the principal handled a relatively delicate and potentially unpleasant situation with compassion and creativity so they were more willing to consider other program adjustments that were mandated by budget cuts.

All of this took quite a bit of the principal's time, but, in the long run it helped establish a climate for deliberate and thoughtful budget reduction. As a result, future budget cuts can be considered and accommodated in less time and with the investment of less emotional energy.

Refine addresses the ways in which schools can reorganize, streamline, or otherwise improve efficiencies without doing harm to the school's core mission and goals. The focus is on finding the most efficient way to achieve goals, rather than fundamentally altering the goals being pursued.

Because most school district budgets are consumed by personnel costs, they often have little flexibility in taking short-term or quick budget reductions. A district in Orange County, California, was faced with budget cuts that needed to come from operating expenses, so just about everything other than personnel was on the table. One of their biggest costs was copying and duplicating—most of which came from the production of consumable instructional materials. At the same time, a district course management software system languished from lack of use by students, teachers, and parents—mostly because there was no sense of urgency for anyone to learn to use it. But the budget cuts changed that.

A major effort was launched to get everyone to use the course management system to distribute instructional materials, instructional resources, and information to parents. It involved both training and marketing—and a lot of help came from the students themselves, most of whom were delighted to move instructional operations to the technological platform that was so important in their lives anyway. Parents were happy because they could check on their child's assignments, grades, and course materials, and could use the system to communicate asynchronously with the teachers.

Training and marketing was the positive, proactive side of this initiative, but everyone also knew that pretty soon the copy machines would be turned off and paper supplies would vanish. That is what ultimately provided the sense of urgency needed to refine the informational, instructional, and communication processes in the district.

Reprioritize deserves special attention because of the complexity of getting people to think, seriously, about the fundamental mission of the school and which of its activities are the most important. Although related to refining school processes, the focus of this activity is on making good decisions about priorities and creating a mechanism for the regular review of priorities as fiscal conditions change.

Demographic changes in a Kansas middle school resulted in a large increase in the number of English Language Learners (ELLs) in a school that had long prided itself on its vast array of exploratory and elective courses. Clearly, the ELL program had to be beefed up, but, because of state-mandated accountability assessments, it couldn't be done at the expense of core academic courses in English, math, science, and social studies. It was obvious, even to people who didn't like the idea, that the only place to find the time for ELL instruction was in the elective curriculum.

But several innovations helped to make the shift in priorities more agreeable to many of the staff members and most of the parents. First, content-based ELL courses were offered in each of the core subject areas— so students got to apply English language skills directly to the specific content of each subject area. Initially, these courses were staffed by a content teacher and an ELL-trained teacher. Ultimately, the goal was to get more content teachers trained in ELL strategies and for the ELL teacher to become a coach to multiple content teachers.

Second, the district purchased high-interest, individually paced language instruction packages for ELL students and provided them with the equipment they needed to use them. In fact, they encouraged students to take the packages home so that the entire family could practice their English, and younger children would be exposed to the language and coached and encouraged by their older siblings.

Finally, a more abbreviated list of elective offerings continued to be provided, but each one had to have a strong ELL component in order for it to be added to the schedule. Eventually, with these modifications, and with continued monitoring, training, and support from the leadership team, the school took on a decidedly ELL focus in all of its offerings.

Regenerate deals with the things that schools can do to generate additional resources or find new sources of funding for innovation and growth. This includes everything from grant-writing to creating productive business/ community partnerships to achieve important school goals and ensure adequate funding for innovative programs and projects.

Sometimes, the alumni of a school can be mobilized to provide both operational support and financial assistance—or even revive a closed or failing school. Two historically African-American high schools in Tampa, Florida, provide examples of what a committed alumni and community can achieve during difficult financial times. Middleton High School was opened in 1934 as a black high school in the district's segregated system. By the mid-1990s, it had been converted to a middle school and fallen into disrepair and a declining achievement spiral. A small group of dedicated alumni began to contact their fellow graduates—many of them outstanding professionals and leading citizens in the Tampa Bay area. This group raised money, public awareness, and commitment to a "new Middleton"—which opened in 2002 as a sophisticated technical institute featuring programs such as Engineering, Computer Game Design, Biotechnology/Biomedical Sciences, and Robotics.

Blake High School, Tampa's other historically black secondary school and Middleton's arch rival since their founding, was not to be outdone by the Middleton alumni. Their alumni group, also comprised of many community leaders, launched an initiative that resulted in the creation of Blake Arts Magnet High School—one of the pre-eminent arts high schools in the southeast. Like Middleton, they were able to secure a spectacular new facility, partly with capital construction funds, but also with significant amounts of grant money and donations secured by and from alumni and other community members. Now, largely because of the high quality of their productions, Blake also earns a substantial portion of its annual budget through ticket sales, community performances, and recordings. From these schools, founded under an ugly system of segregation and impoverishment, have emerged two of the most accomplished high schools in the region—largely because of powerful alumni and community support and through the efforts of enlightened district leaders and school board members.

More Good News

These stories are just a few of dozens we have heard from school leaders across the nation. All of them confronted, and continue to confront, harsh economic realities that dramatically affect their schools and their educational programs. But educators are also smart and devoted to the kids they serve, so once the shock of a reduced base budget wears off, and grieving for the school as they once knew it is over, these dedicated professionals apply knowledge, hard work, tenacity, and a generous helping of innovation not only to cope with the New Normal, but to prosper and take their schools to new levels of service and achievement.

The rest of this book explores each of the Four *R*'s in detail with a special focus on the strategies, plans, and tools that effective school leaders use to provide effective leadership in an era of declining resources. We also include real-world examples and stories from school leaders, like you, who work every day to deliver high-quality education and student services that far exceed the value of the money they are provided.

Think About It

Take a few minutes to think about how your own school has changed over the past decade in its demographics, enrollment, base budget, and expectations for accountability. Think about the way the school has responded to those changes and how successful those changes have been. Now, spend some time thinking about what you think you could or should be doing to respond to these changes, and what financial, organizational, or other resources you would need to make them. To launch this conversation in your own school, use this exercise with your leadership team, team leaders, and department heads as a stimulus for a discussion on future directions for the school.

How has your school changed in the past 10 years?	That was then . . .	This is now . . .	What have we done about this change?	What could or should we do?
Community and student demographics?				
Enrollment?				
Base budget?				
Accountability?				
Other areas?				

Now Try This

Create your own learning community.

1. Make a call list of colleague-leaders you know and mark your calendar to call each of them once a month to find out how they are responding to emerging challenges in your region and to share ideas from your own school. You might even suggest that you all get together for breakfast or dinner once in a while to sustain a network of sharing and learning that will benefit everyone.

2. Use technology to create your own personal learning network (PLN). Start with Eric Sheninger's "A Principal's Reflections" blog (http://esheninger.blogspot.com), your local, state, or national principals' organization blogs, or by joining a broad-based learning network such as edWeb.net (www.edweb.net/).

3. Tweet-Follow-Retweet. Find several micro-bloggers on Twitter and follow their tweets. Compile a list of Twitter accounts from your staff, and retweet good ideas that come to your attention. To begin, try some of these very active Tweeting principals and organizations: Smart Brief on Education (@SBEducation), Eric Sheninger (@NMHS_Principal), Scott McLeod (@mcleod), Routledge Education (@RoutledgeEd), Edutopia (@edutopia), and Howard and Ron, the authors, (@practical_leadr).

Leadership in Action

Check out how these school leaders have met the challenges in their own schools.

1. Ginsburg, R., & Multon, K. (2011, May 10). Leading through a fiscal nightmare: The impact on superintendents and principals. *Education Week*. Retrieved from www.edweek.org/ew/articles/2011/05/10/kap pan_ginsberg.html

    An outstanding study of how the fiscal crisis affects school leaders and what some of them have done about it.

2. Santos, F. (2011, August 17). Lessons in austerity: How city principals make budgets work. *New York Times*. Retrieved from www.nytimes.com/2011/08/18/nyregion/five-new-york-city-school-principals-talk-budget-cuts.html?pagewanted=all

   An interesting take on budget cuts from principals in a system that has little flexibility in how they can move their money around.

3. Education World. (n.d.). Budgets pose multiple choice dilemma for administrators. *Educationworld.com*. Retrieved from www.educationworld.com/a_admin/admin306.shtml

   With fewer and fewer items that can be cut from school budgets, how are some school leaders making the best of a bad situation that is only likely to get worse in the foreseeable future?

Leading and Prospering in the New Normal Environment

Every school in the country is struggling with a new reality. Expectations for student achievement are higher than ever, even in the most successful schools. At the same time, resources, both human and financial, are stable at best and in most cases declining.

This new reality has forced leaders to look at their programs and often make tough choices about what can be sustained. Too often that appears to be a forced choice between programs uniquely aligned with the needs of students and the need to cut costs.

Many school leaders have seen this challenge as an opportunity, an opportunity to question long-standing practices and create a "new reality" that maintains the vigor and vitality of a quality school.

Over the past few years we've worked with school leaders in all sorts of settings, rural, suburban, and urban, as they've faced this challenge. What we've discovered is that the leaders that were most successful shared a set of beliefs.

Anchored in Beliefs

Leaders were committed to a collaborative process to confront their "new reality." District constraints and parameters were universally clear—limit or reduce expenditures. But there was also recognition throughout the school of the importance of ownership and support for any program changes or new initiatives. In each case the work was anchored in these four principles.

- **Begin with Clear Goals**—Schools that were most successful adapting to the New Normal were those where the leader recognized the importance of being clear about the mission of the school. Programs are merely tools, tools that teachers and principals can use to impact student learning. A school is rarely successful at improving instruction by simply changing the organization. They are far more successful when they take time to clearly identify the goals they hope to achieve and to use those goals to guide decisions about program changes.

- **Challenge Long-Standing Norms**—Long-standing assumptions about the organization and operation of a school can inhibit creativity and limit alternatives. Leaders who were most adept at responding to the New Normal were those who did not defend the status quo but instead were comfortable questioning current practices, identifying alternatives, and refocusing on a shared vision.

- **Value Collaboration**—Nothing provokes a stronger reaction than trying to impose program change. Successful leaders were those who understood the value of using an inclusive process to clarify values, identify goals, and consider alternatives. Every plan benefits from the discussion generated when stakeholders are included in the planning. They also found it useful to agree on norms the group will use to identify alternatives and make decisions.

- **Listen to All Points-of-View**—It's also important to assure that different points-of-view are included in the discussion. Leaders who were open to differing perspectives but comfortable questioning and challenging every suggestion to ensure that it is anchored in research and best practice were often the most successful adapting to the New Normal.

Part II will discuss leadership in the New Normal. It will identify those competencies and skills evident in leaders who successfully navigated this environment.

2 Critical Role of Leadership in the New Normal Environment

School leaders hold one of the most complex jobs in our society. They are pulled in many different directions while expected to be thoughtful decision makers, expert personnel managers, stern student disciplinarians, engaging public relations specialists, and skillful budget managers.

In challenging economic times leaders often find themselves needing to balance conflicting but equally valid priorities. The times call for bold leadership, leadership that has a clear vision for their school or district and the capacity to work with diverse constituent groups to maintain a focus on quality educational experiences for every student.

This chapter will discuss the role of leadership in the New Normal. We believe that no school or district will be successful in these times unless they are lead by a thoughtful and skilled leader. A Michigan principal we know said, "Almost anyone can lead when there's lots of money, programs and staff. But when times get tough you quickly find out whether you have the stamina to lead."

The most successful leaders are those who have a vision for their school or district but who recognize the importance of welcoming stakeholders into the discussion about vision; and leaders are most successful when they have both the knowledge and skills to set priorities based on the vision, to think more deeply about collaboration, to embrace a more entrepreneurial approach, to build connections and advocate for their school or district, and to build and energize among others a belief that, even in challenging times, all things are possible when good people work together.

School Leadership That Works

One of the most comprehensive analyses of the effect of leadership is the work of Marzano, Waters, and McNulty (2005). They looked at years of studies on leadership and identified 21 responsibilities associated with effective leadership. Our goal is not to recite the 21 responsibilities but rather to focus on the deeper meaning of their work.

First Order or Second Order

Marzano and his colleagues described two approaches that seemed to underlie the success of the 21 responsibilities. They were first-order change, a gradual more subtle approach to making change, and second-order change, involving more dramatic approaches and innovative thinking.

First-Order Change—First-order change is pretty much doing what you're already doing but making relatively minor adjustments. For example, to control costs you might reduce the number of classes available to students or you might eliminate transportation for high school students.

First-order change as described by Marzano et al. is "more incremental" (2005, p. 66), that is, it is moving to the next logical extension of your current program.

Second-Order Change—Second-order change is far more substantive and certainly not incremental. It occurs when you choose, or are forced to choose, to do something fundamentally different than what you've been doing. This sort of change often transforms the organization in ways that cannot be easily undone. For example, you might choose to partner with neighboring districts to invest in a distance learning program increasing the offerings available to students. Or you might redesign the school day so that students are involved in varied learning activities, some online, some face-to-face, some on-campus, and some not. This redesign changes the relationships among students and teachers and embraces a changing notion of what constitutes teaching and learning.

Another way to think of the differences between first- and second-order change is that when first-order changes are made, an organization often continues to look at the problem from its current perspective, from a discussion about what has worked in the past. This approach is often about using strategies that have been successful, or unsuccessful, in the past rather than deploying different approaches.

Leadership in Action

Sweet Home High School is located in a logging community in the foothills of the Oregon Cascades. Traditionally many students completed high school and immediately went to work in the timber industry. But the reality of the New Normal is that there are fewer and fewer jobs in this industry and those that remain require more education and the ability to use various forms of technology.

Keith Winslow became principal in 2012 and went to work changing the climate of the school. It had been plagued by poor attendance and a lack of student engagement. As a result of Keith's work, there is a greater emphasis on providing all students with a rigorous academic experience and an expectation that all students will enroll in a post-secondary educational program. That's quite a change for Sweet Home.

In his first year as principal, he worked with staff to secure a grant from an Oregon foundation to support converting a portion of the campus into a commons area where students can relax during lunch and before and after school. Tables with stools were added along with comfortable chairs you might find in any coffee shop. It's located adjacent to a school store selling school supplies and souvenirs. Next to the store an office has been converted into a yogurt shop selling six flavors of frozen yogurt. The first day the yogurt shop opened it made $132. The funds from these activities are used to support the school's college readiness program including visits to college campuses and acquisition of resource materials.

Keith describes the commons as a "real success." "We learned that by changing something like this we changed the climate of the school. Who could have imagined. We trusted our students and they responded. We asked them to act like adults, and they do."

Second-order change occurs when you look at problems differently. You conceptualize the problem in new ways often describing it differently than in the past and you identify or create new strategies for addressing the problem. This approach often expands the range of options and the way people in your organization think about issues.

The New Normal requires that leaders think differently about their school and strategies for ensuring effective student learning. This new thinking is more closely associated with second-order changes than with first order. The most successful leaders are those who challenge the regularities and long-standing norms of their school. They are comfortable embracing new and innovative approaches to serving students, and they thrive in an environment where the unexpected has become the norm.

Think About It

Look at this blog post about second-order change written by Greg Miller, a principal in Toronto. How do you react to how his school changed the learning environment? http://gregmillerprincipal.com/tag/second-order-change/

Choosing First- or Second-Order Change

When solving problems, particularly in times of stress, people often look at every problem as one requiring first-order change. All of us tend to use the strategies and tools with which we are familiar and to rely on tested approaches to resolve problems. So, when resources are reduced, a common response is to look at the budget and find programs and people to be eliminated or reduced.

Such an approach can often be detrimental to the success of the organization because it assumes that by simply doing less you can stay within the budget and be successful. Often, just the opposite approach is required. You must think about how to nurture, sustain, and grow your school's program. To do so requires thinking about the problem in starkly different ways.

Setting aside our predispositions about how to solve problems is one of the most challenging leadership issues. As Fullan (2001) noted, "The big problems of the day are complex, rife with paradoxes and dilemmas. For these problems, there are no once-and-for-all answers" (p. 73).

Our natural inclination to approach change by looking at issues through our prior experience can be detrimental to success in the New Normal. The failure to recognize the importance of looking at issues differently becomes a significant barrier to achieving the success needed in today's schools.

Think About It

Think about the changes that you've made or anticipate making. List those that are first-order changes, and those that are second-order changes.

First-Order Changes	Second-Order Changes

Final Thoughts

When confronted by the reality of reduced funding and fewer human resources many school leaders choose to make incremental adjustments to their budgets. Other leaders see the New Normal as an opportunity to reconsider the school's core mission and how it serves students.

Those are starkly different approaches. Choosing to merely "tinker" with the program or to embrace the New Normal is a reflection of whether a principal is comfortable with first-order change or willing to make the more substantive changes described as second-order change.

Resources

The Marzano Center site provides additional information about the research behind Marzano, Waters, and McNulty's (2005) Leadership Model.

www.marzanocenter.com/Leadership-Evaluation/

First- and Second-Order Change—A short summary of the differences between first- and second-order change.

http://internationalschoolleadership.wikispaces.com/file/detail/Marzano+Second+Order+change.pdf

Leadership Competencies and Skills for the New Normal Environment

In Chapter 2 we discussed the important role of leadership in the New Normal. We've found that the most successful leaders in this environment are those who see this new reality as an opportunity for their school or district to refocus its efforts on providing students a quality educational experience. They are predisposed to embrace change and to recognize the importance of using these circumstances to strengthen and improve their school or district.

This chapter will look at the competencies and skills required of leaders in the New Normal. A competency is a set of personal characteristics like values, motives, and attitudes that a leader holds. Competencies have been described as the superset of skills that makes a person able to complete a task or fulfill the requirements of a job. For example, if you are a good problem solver (a competency), several skills are required to solve a problem (the ability to define the problem, knowledge to generate possible solutions, and behavior that allows you to make a decision).

A skill, on the other hand, is a specific, technical ability to perform a task. We'll also look at the specific skills a leader needs to be successful in this new environment.

We find the work of Marzano, Waters, and McNulty (2005) compelling because of the thoughtful analysis of multiple studies on leadership. Their reliance on research strengthened their analysis. We're also struck by the thoughtful work of Public Impact (2008), a educational policy consulting firm from North Carolina working for the Chicago Public Education Fund. Their report identified the competencies of successful school turnaround leaders. But more importantly they identified specific descriptors of each competency. Both reports informed our analysis.

The Same But Different

In the New Normal, leaders continue to have responsibilities similar to those they had previously. What's different is the context in which they do their work and the need to view their work through a slightly different lens.

In Chapter 1 we described the leadership challenge, the reality that the context in which schools operate continues to change in bold and dramatic ways. These changes mean that leaders must deploy their competencies and skills in ways that may be unfamiliar and slightly uncomfortable, and that may require innovative and imaginative thinking.

Leadership Competencies

Successful leaders are . . .

Visionary—They partner with others in their organization and community to create a shared vision for their school. They recognize the importance of having a vision of the future and where they want their school to be in the future. They can imagine the possibilities and how their school can thrive in this new environment.

Inspirational—They are skilled at energizing employees, families, and the community to embrace changes and to see the New Normal as an opportunity rather than a challenge.

Strategic—They understand the strengths and challenges in their organization and are skilled at identifying ways to leverage their strengths and partner to address their challenges.

Disciplined—They are focused on achieving their shared vision and recognize the importance of aligning every school activity with the vision. They identify ways to make their organization more efficient, and more successful, without losing sight of its vision.

Confident—They are resolute in their focus because they work closely with employees, families, and community and respect the commitment to their shared vision. Their confidence helps others imagine the possibilities in this New Normal.

Action-oriented—Just as they are disciplined, they also understand the importance of action. They are not impulsive but are disposed to action

---

rather than reaction. They adopt a "whatever it takes" stance regardless of the challenges faced in this new environment.

Decisive—They recognize the need to make decisions but make them in support of the school's vision. They value information and input but are clear about outcomes.

Ethical—They lead based on clear ethical principles and recognize the importance of doing the 'right thing' rather than the most attractive option. This may mean abandoning or altering past practice so that resources are used to support student learning.

Visionary

Perhaps nothing is more important for a leader than to hold a clear sense of vision for their school. A leader must possess their own personal vision and be committed to working collaboratively with teachers, staff, families, and community to develop a clear and compelling vision for their school.

It is far too easy to think of vision as a few short statements drafted by a committee, posted on a wall and then forgotten. Leaders who possess real vision recognize that being visionary requires deep, thoughtful, deliberation about the future of their school.

Visionary leaders start with a clear personal vision. Personal vision is important because it reflects one's values and beliefs, it can identify priorities in one's life and it provides guidance about what is most important and how you want to spend your time.

Each of us is shaped by a unique set of experiences in our lives—people we meet, places we go, challenges we face, events we attend. These experiences shape our personal ethic (Shapiro & Stefkovich, 2011). Our ethic consists of the most fundamental beliefs we hold about life, work, and our relationships with people.

Visionary leaders recognize the people and events that shaped their lives and contributed to the formation of their personal ethic and personal vision. They understand how that ethic shapes our work and the decisions we make.

Think About It

Take a few minutes and reflect on your life. What experiences have you had that are so powerful they shape your personal ethic?

- Describe one or two people who helped shape your personal ethics and beliefs.
- Identify two or three events that occurred during your lifetime and shaped your beliefs.

Visionary leaders have a clear personal vision. But they recognize that schools are most successful when there is a commitment by employees, families, and community to a shared vision.

While clear about their own beliefs, visionary leaders understand the importance of facilitating work with employees, family, and community to share aspirations and develop a shared vision that reflects the diverse views of the community. Visionary leaders are skilled at listening to others and building connections between the individual aspirations of community members and the school's vision.

A visionary leader looks like this . . .

They . . .

- understand the importance of a clear vision to guide their school
- are skilled at monitoring and anticipating the issues and trends that will impact schools
- are good at imagining a future in response to these issues and trends
- generate ideas and alternatives in response to the changing environment
- communicate their beliefs and vision in formal and informal conversations

---

Now Try This

Think about your work as a leader and then rate yourself on each of the following behaviors.

1. I can describe my personal vision for my school.

2. I'm comfortable exploring the diverse points-of-view in my school community.

3. I'm able to facilitate a process to develop a shared vision for our school that is shaped by my own personal vision and the diverse perspectives in my school community.
4. I routinely talk about my personal vision for our school.

Inspirational

Inspirational leaders motivate everyone in their school to get onboard and support the vision. Teachers and other school staff, families, and students are passionate about their commitment to the vision and to making their school a successful place to work and to learn.

The most successful inspirational leaders lead in many different ways. They may be charismatic, but most often are not. Instead they inspire through their words and their actions. Leading by example, they rally employees as well as families and community to work together to ensure a quality educational experience for their students and children.

Inspirational leaders are good at bringing others to their point-of-view. They understand how to motivate people using logic, reason, emotion, and persuasion. They're not intimidating, dogmatic, or unyielding. But they are clear about their beliefs, about the vision for their school and they speak from his or her heart.

Part of being an inspirational leader is recognizing the importance of good interpersonal skills. Inspirational leaders have a high degree of emotional intelligence, a high level of finesse, and are passionate about what they do.

Leadership in Action

When Richard Barajas became principal of Milby High School in Houston, he immediately recognized the need to motivate and inspire his staff. Milby is located in one of the most impoverished parts of Houston and serves many first-generation immigrant families. He found that many of his staff were disillusioned by poor attendance characterized by some students leaving school mid-way through the day. Test scores and graduation rates were low.

Richard, who grew up in the neighborhood his school served, immediately began to work with teacher leaders to identify strategies to turn things around. He talked with students and discovered that most students leaving during the day were actually going to work so that they could help support their family. He worked with departments to provide collaborative time to work on improving instruction and developing common assessments. He got the district to agree to an extended school day so that students could begin as early as 7 a.m. and then leave for work. Others could arrive later in the morning after fulfilling child-care obligations and take classes until 5 p.m.

Most importantly Richard was an advocate for his students. He talked about their accomplishments, academic, athletic, and personal. He worked with families to build their support, and he identified resources in the community that would help students fund their post-secondary education.

An inspirational leader looks like this . . .

They . . .

- value individuals and their contributions
- treat others with respect, trust, and dignity
- model positive interpersonal skills
- act in ways that make people willing to follow
- recognize the importance of developing others

Strategic

Strategic leaders understand the strengths and challenges in their organization. They recognize threats and opportunities, and they are skilled at identifying ways to leverage their school's strengths.

These leaders understand the importance of building alliances often with individuals or groups that may not traditionally be connected to schools. They recognize that through alliances they can create opportunities for their school and its students.

Every community has a set of "movers and shakers," those individuals who are recognized leaders, the people others turn to for guidance on important issues. They are often recognized for their ability to rally support, identify resources, and build coalitions. Often they don't have formal leadership roles. They may even be the people sitting in the coffee shop every morning discussing local and world events. What characterizes them is their ability to mold and shape public opinion.

Leadership in Action

At Yoncalla Elementary School principal Jerry Fauci envisioned a community greenhouse on campus where students could have experiential learning. But the school district lacked the resources to build and maintain such a structure. He approached nearby individuals and businesses who shared his vision. Most importantly, he knew "who" to talk with, who could marshal the support to make the greenhouse a reality. Working with a local coffee-shop owner, he was introduced to others in the community who contributed funds, but also materials to construct the greenhouse. Today it sits proudly next to the school's athletic fields; and students plant seeds, transplant seedlings, care for the plants, and harvest the crops. It's a marvelous hands-on experience for students, one achieved by knowing who to talk with and how to strategically build alliances.

School leaders who are most strategic are those who recognize the importance of being an advocate for their school, of building alliances with individuals and groups, and building strong lines of communication.

A strategic leader looks like this . . .

They . . .

- value the importance of open, honest communication
- advocate for their school in their community
- recognize the importance of building alliances and partnerships
- are good at seeing patterns and links between activities and groups

Now Try This

Think about your own school and community. Make a list of the "movers and shakers," those people who have a unique ability to influence public opinion. How might you use them in any advocacy efforts on behalf of your school?

Disciplined

Disciplined leaders are unwavering in their commitment to their school's vision. They are focused on achieving the vision and set out to do so. While recognizing obstacles, disciplined leaders are comfortable confronting those challenges and identifying ways to minimize them.

Disciplined leaders are also good tacticians. They are guided by the bottom-line (the school's vision) and thrive on data about their school. At the same time, they don't feel constrained by the data but rather use it to help identify direction and opportunities.

A disciplined leader looks like this . . .

They . . .

- maintain focus on the school or district vision and mission
- are patient and cool-headed when faced with challenges
- expect data to be used to guide decision making
- focus on the problem, rather than the people involved, when they encounter difficulty
- see challenges as opportunities to learn and try new things rather than as insurmountable barriers

---

Now Try This

Think about a time when you encountered serious obstacles to implementing a school improvement initiative. How did you respond to the challenge? In retrospect, what advice would you offer yourself about your response?

Leadership in Action

Five years ago Scott Read became principal of Taft High School in Lincoln City, Oregon. Taft serves a diverse community with many students from modest-income families. Due to the economy and declining enrollments, Taft was reducing staff, eliminating professional development, and narrowing elective choices for students. Both test scores and graduation rates needed improvement. Committed to improving student achievement among all students, Scott embarked on a plan to adopt a proficiency-based learning model in core classes. Despite initial resistance from the staff, Scott persisted. He identified indicators of success and monitored them religiously. They adopted a four-day week schedule, and students not meeting proficiency were required to attend on Friday mornings. Friday afternoon was used for their own professional learning. More importantly, Scott had a "laser-like" focus on improving student learning and ensuring that students became proficient in core content areas. This disciplined focus has resulted in improved test scores, improved graduation rates, and high college acceptance rates.

Confident

Successful school leaders are confident. When we talk about confidence we mean that they are clear about their own beliefs, about the school's vision and mission, and about their commitment to success.

Confident leaders are also humble. They treat others with respect, trust, and dignity. They are always considerate of the needs and feelings of others, and they value a culture that values individuals and their individual contributions while being collaborative and productive.

Clarity of vision helps leaders exude a confidence in their work and the decision they make. It sustains them when they face challenging issues.

A confident leader looks like this . . .

They . . .
- have a personal, but humble, belief in their own ability
- are realistic about the opportunities and challenges facing their organization
- remain visibly focused on their work

Action-Oriented

A bias for action characterizes successful leaders in this new environment. While committed to a collegial and collaborative school these leaders recognize the importance of taking action that will improve the educational experience of students. They don't make excuses like "we don't have the resources" or "there's fewer staff."

Even though they are predisposed to responding, these leaders also recognize the need to abandon practices that may not have achieved the desired results, or to change direction based on new or updated information.

Leadership in Action

Jay Mathieson is principal of La Pine (OR) High School and Oregon's principal of the year for 2011. La Pine, is a blue-collar logging town, located 30 miles south of Bend and part of the Bend–La Pine School District. Many students are from low-income families and many traditionally went to work immediately after high school. Jay loves to immerse himself in data and the wall of his office had multi-year trends on several key indicators—achievement tests, graduation rates, attendance, and suspension rates.

Having a bias for action Jay made the data public so that it became an item of discussion in both formal and informal meetings with teacher leaders and his staff. Rather than make accusations or threats Jay challenged his staff to improve the data.

Together they identified the training and other resources they needed. They identified benchmarks they would monitor and they worked together to monitor gains, identify needed improvements, and refine the plan.

There was no option to do nothing. At La Pine High School, Jay Mathieson was committed to a "do whatever it takes" approach and his commitment to working collaboratively with his staff resulted in significant gains on every indicator.

An action-oriented leader looks like this . . .

They . . .

- are comfortable gathering and using data to guide decisions
- tolerate ambiguity well
- recognize the need to adjust plans in response to changing conditions
- effectively handle disagreements and conflicts in order to maintain momentum

Decisive

The most successful leaders are not those who necessarily make quick decisions. Decisive leaders are those who recognize when "shooting from the hip" may be detrimental to their school. Following Theodore Roosevelt's advice is always appropriate—"In any moment of decision, the best thing you can do is the right thing, the next best thing is the wrong thing, and the worst thing you can do is nothing" (Blaydes, 2003, p. 136).

Decisive leaders welcome feedback. They encourage feedback about their personal performance, about the school's direction, and about ways to continue to improve. "Seeking continuous improvement in their [schools], they also seek it for themselves" (Frank, 2005).

A decisive leader looks like this . . .

They . . .

- routinely monitor their school's progress
- identify and respond to outside forces that may impact their school
- are analytical thinkers
- are skilled at defining problems
- use data and other information to shape alternatives and strategies
- are focused on results

Ethical

John Dewey (1902) described ethics as one's conduct involving decisions about right or wrong. The dilemma for school leaders is "right or wrong" according to whom? Or "right and wrong," as approved by whom?

Ethical leaders recognize the complexity of today's society and the diverse ethical perspectives present in that society (Shapiro & Stefkovich, 2011). But more importantly ethical leaders understand the origin of their own personal ethic and those people and events that have shaped who they are and what they believe.

Ethical leaders are clear in what they believe and use their personal ethic to guide their work and shape their decisions. They are comfortable talking about their ethic and the forces that have shaped it. But they are also reluctant to impose their ethical beliefs on others. Rather, they are comfortable talking about the diverse set of ethics present in any school community. They look for the commonalities present in diverse ethics. For example, a high school principal in northern Michigan talked with his staff about the origin of his own personal ethic. He shared his upbringing, his experience in the military, and the challenges finding care for aging parents. He encouraged every member of his staff to think about their own personal journey. At the next staff meeting some teachers shared their own experiences. Together the staff identified their own "staff ethic," those things that guide their work with students and with their families and community. This principal reported, "the discussion about beliefs moved our work to a different level. We used to point fingers at people with whom we didn't agree. Now we're focused on our common beliefs. That really has helped to provide focus for our work."

An ethical leader looks like this . . .

They . . .

- recognize the people and experiences who shaped their beliefs
- are clear about their own beliefs
- understand how beliefs guide decisions they make
- appreciate the diversity of points-of-view present in any school community
- are comfortable talking about beliefs and how they shape action

---

Assess Your Leadership Competency

Use the description of the 8 leadership competencies to assess your own leadership.

1. Rate yourself from 1 (area of need) to 10 (proficient) in each area.

2. Total your score and assess your leadership competency.

3. Use the scores to create a personal development plan. You may want to identify a mentor, or participate in professional development or some other growth activity.

4. Most important is to leverage your strengths.

Competency	My Rating (1 to 10)
1. Visionary	_____
2. Inspirational	_____
3. Strategic	_____

4. Disciplined	_____
5. Confident	_____
6. Action-Oriented	_____
7. Decisive	_____
8. Ethical	_____

My Total Score: _____

My Strengths:

My Opportunities for Growth:

Final Thoughts

Good leaders are present in all types of organizations and all kinds of settings. But during a time of stable or declining resources, exceptional leaders emerge because of their clear vision, their steadfast commitment to student learning, and their unwavering willingness to act in ethical and strategic ways to make their school a place where students and staff continue to learn and grow.

Resources

Forbes Article on "Top 10 Qualities That Make a Great Leader" (2012)

www.forbes.com/sites/tanyaprive/2012/12/19/top-10-qualities-that-make-a-great-leader/

HR World—"Top 10 Leadership Qualities"—David Hakala (2008)

www.hrworld.com/features/top-10-leadership-qualities-031908/

Leading for Learning: Reflective Tools for Schools and District Leaders (2003)

Center for the Study of Teaching and Policy

http://depts.washington.edu/ctpmail/PDFs/LforLSummary-02-03.pdf

4 Changing Leader Roles

There are probably more books and papers written about leadership than almost any other topic, hundreds of them about school leadership. This chapter is not an attempt to share a new model or provide a new list of leadership traits and characteristics. There are plenty of those available in other places.

What we do want to share is what we've learned distilling the literature on effective school leadership and working with dozens of principals who are grappling with this New Normal environment.

This chapter will discuss the changing roles of school leaders as they deal with this "new" environment. We'll provide examples where appropriate and examine how leaders have adapted to the New Normal.

The New Normal

Educators and policy makers have debated whether or not money makes a difference in student learning and success. Some suggest that additional resources are needed to strengthen programs and services. Others just as passionately contend that there is no evidence that additional resources make a difference (Walberg, 2011).

This chapter will not debate this issue. Rather we will look at how school leaders responded when faced by the challenges of reduced or stable resources. Schools in every state are confronted with the need to make budget reductions and to carefully examine expenditures. In most cases, reductions have occurred for several years and are now a routine part of the annual budgeting process. As a result of the current financial environment the easiest, least disruptive, reductions have already taken place. Further reductions will require a more complex process of assessing the contribution of every function to the core mission of schools and balancing competing interests.

There is no single process that makes decisions in the New Normal easy. Because there are many interest groups in a school community, all with a vested interest in the district's programs and practices, the process is often highly politicized. Bolman and Deal (2008) suggest that organizations are most political when confronted by scarce resources like money. The tension around budgets and resource allocation, in a very politicized environment, leads to conflict among groups. The result is intense bargaining, negotiating, and jockeying for position to minimize the impact on favored programs.

The Same but Different

So, how do leaders respond in this new environment? Does their role change or does it remain the same?

We've discovered that the role of the principal is quite stable. The issues are often the same from year to year. What changes is the context in which the issues emerge. So, discussions about the use of resources are more frequently about efficiency, innovation, flexibility, and sustainability rather than expansion and growth. The set of tools leaders use are the same. What's different is that those tools are used in very different ways.

We've identified five areas where the role is familiar, but the application quite different.

- **Vision**—Successful school leaders are those who help their organizations imagine an attractive future where regardless of resource issues they are able to achieve their goals and make a difference for students. The New Normal requires leaders to create a future that may be far different than the present. This requires skills to help their community support this reality.

- **Improve Instruction**—This remains the primary role of a school leader. The "new" environment means that schools are expected to achieve better results with students at the same time they adapt to the availability of fewer resources. Successful school leaders will identify time for collaboration, for professional learning, and for innovative instruction despite resource constraints.

- **Problem Solver**—Principals have always been problem solvers. But in this "new" environment they are expected to be far more analytical, far more creative, and increasingly comfortable challenging the status quo. Rather than reacting, the most successful leaders will anticipate issues and work to creatively design and implement solutions.

- **Advocacy**—Public relations and advocacy remain an important role for school leaders but this "new" environment requires that the leader be a skilled communicator, a builder of alliances and partnerships, and a forceful advocate for their school. The role of advocate is not merely public relations. It recognizes the need to share the "message" about your school's vision and to work with interest groups, inside and outside of the school, to achieve that vision.

- **Collaboration**—Collaborative skills are essential for any contemporary leader but no more so than when they are faced with the need to negotiate among competing interests to build support for your school. Leaders must have a whole set of collaborative tools that they can deploy to facilitate the work of groups, to guide discussion, and to help make decisions.

A discussion of the competencies and skills needed by leaders in this New Normal was provided in Chapter 3. Here we provide short vignettes that illustrate how five practicing school leaders used their skills at visioning, improving instruction, problem-solving, advocacy, and collaboration.

Visionary Leadership

Tom Horn arrived at Al Kennedy Alternative High School with little experience working in schools but a real commitment to serving students that are often marginalized in traditional schools. Kennedy was considered the "last chance" for students who had not been successful in other schools in the South Lane School District in western Oregon.

A school of about 80 with more than 90% qualifying for free or reduced lunch and 65% recognized as homeless, Kennedy is focused on building relationships with students while working on academic success.

Tom quickly recognized the need for Kennedy to not look like any traditional school. His vision was to build a unique program with a curriculum focused on sustainability issues in agriculture, architecture, and climate change. Ecological responsibility, as well as social responsibility, would be emphasized.

The Kennedy program is anchored in six core beliefs that reflect a commitment to active, engaged learning.

- Learning should be a fascinating adventure, a rigorous but joyful pursuit.
- Each individual has natural talents and intellectual aptitudes.
- Cooperation and teamwork are essential to a sustainable society.
- Learning is an energetic pursuit.
- True learning calls on every facet of the human mind, heart, and body.
- Learning is the doorway to the wonders of culture, the natural work, and the community.

Implementing the vision required the formation of partnerships with individuals and groups. In a community with a long history in the timber industry, this could be a challenge. Tom contacted local, state, and regional agencies to share his vision and to talk about his students. He made presentations. He drove miles to meetings. He spent hours of his own time designing and redesigning programs.

His efforts resulted in partnerships with AmeriCorps, the U.S. Forest Service, nonprofits like the Coast Fork Willamette Watershed Council and Oregon Green Schools. He even partnered with Weyerhaeuser Corporation and several local businesses.

Part of what makes the Kennedy program unique is that students go into the community to both learn and apply their learning. The school has partnerships with the Bureau of Land Management, the City of Cottage Grove, and the U.S. Forest Service. Students work on projects related to their school studies and enjoy giving back to their community.

The Kennedy campus is unlike most high school campuses. There is a row of beehives tended by students. The former athletic fields are the site of sustainable gardens where students grow vegetables they donate to local food cooperatives and food banks. They even raise tilapia to donate to food kitchens. In another part of the campus students build a canoe that they will use on a spring float trip on the nearby Willamette River, where they study environmental issues and water quality. Elsewhere students work on a plan to restore wetlands near a local landfill.

Tom Horn and his vision transformed Al Kennedy Alternative High School and changed the future for many of his students. Last year 42% were enrolled in college courses through a nearby community college, another partner. Dropout rates have fallen and test scores, while still low, have risen dramatically. The Kennedy model is unique but illustrates how one leader, during challenging times, can transform a school through the power of their vision.

Tom Horn recently moved to another school, but Mike Ingham, the current principal, continues the sustainability program. Additional information about Al Kennedy Alternative School is available at http://blogs.slane.k12. or.us/kennedy/.

Instructional Leadership

Cottage Grove High School in the Willamette Valley of Oregon has struggled the past five years with regular reductions in resources. Each year the budget was reduced, and teachers who retired or left the school were not replaced. In fact, no new teachers have been hired for six years.

A logging community, Cottage Grove struggled as demand for timber products declined and unemployment increased. The high school is the pride of the community and is housed in a building less than 10 years old. Approximately 750 students attend the school, 60% qualifying for free or reduced lunch, 15% for special education services.

The staff prides itself on the success of their students. Cottage Grove currently has average daily attendance of 92% and a graduation rate of 87%, significant improvement over prior years.

Kay Graham was hired as principal of the high school in 2010 and immediately recognized the need, despite resource cuts, to find ways to strengthen and enhance their instructional program. Kay worked with her leadership team to adopt both reading and writing across the curriculum. She secured funding from a state grant and local sources to support a modest professional development program using regional experts. Freshman and sophomore students loop with the same teacher for both years. During that time they focus on essential literacy skills. Juniors and seniors focus on college and career readiness as well as interventions for those needing additional support.

Central to the success at Cottage Grove was agreement among the staff to use common vocabulary when talking with students about writing. Their TEA Paragraph (Topic Sentence, Evidence, Analysis) became something recognized by every student and was used by teachers in every class including foreign language and elective classes.

Funding was secured from local businesses for a summer reading program. Every rising ninth and tenth grader receives a high-interest paperback book that they are expected to read during the summer. Their language arts teachers use that book at the beginning of the school year to immediately focus students on reading and writing.

Kay Graham and the Cottage Grove High School staff did not allow budget reductions and the loss of resources like professional development and supplies inhibit their commitment to improving the literacy skills of their students. Everything described in this vignette was achieved with no additional district funds.

Additional information about Cottage Grove High School can be obtained at http://blogs.slane.k12.or.us/cghs/.

Problem Solving

At Park Junior High in LaGrange (IL) School District 102 there was a need to find ways to reduce expenditures and more efficiently utilize the teaching staff. Park serves approximately 620 students in grades 7–8 but enrollment has been steady or declining.

Rather than react to budget constraints District 102 organized a planning group of teachers, administrators, and parents to review the Park program; examine data about it's successes and challenges; and agree on a statement of mission and vision for the school.

The following year a similar group met to examine how to modify the schedule to reduce staffing issues and improve the learning environment. More than a dozen alternatives were identified but the one selected reduced costs and positioned Park to address the needs of students in the 21st century, anticipating implementation of Common Core standards. The new schedule provided longer instructional blocks (two class periods) for all core content areas (Mathematics, Reading/Language Arts, Science, Social

Studies). Mathematics and Reading/Language Arts meet daily for a double block. Science and Social Studies meet on alternate days for a double block. Teams consist of two mathematics and two reading/language arts teachers along with one science and one social studies teacher.

A key goal to provide each core content area with additional instructional minutes was met. By creating longer instructional blocks and having some classes meet on alternate days, having fewer passing periods, and from modifying the exploratory program captured some of the time.

Park's "new" exploratory program was perhaps its most defining characteristic. Its four exploratory classes, art, music, health and STEM, were no longer stand-alone classes taken everyday for a semester. Instead each content area was linked to one of the core subjects and integrated with that content. For example, the seventh grade STEM was integrated into mathematics and music was integrated into language arts. Eighth grade art was integrated into language arts and health into mathematics.

The summer prior to implementation, exploratory teachers designed learning modules that met state curricular standards. The modules were taught in the core content class and intentional links were made between the exploratory subject and the core content. The emphasis was application of their learning to "real world" situations.

Park's innovative schedule achieved its goal of cost savings and rationalizing the schedule for both students and teachers. It responded to the learning needs of their students and authentically linked exploratory subjects with students' learning in other core subjects, a "real world" application for their learning.

Additional information about Park Junior High can be retrieved at its website (www.dist102.k12.il.us/schools/park-junior-high).

Advocacy

Located in eastern Oregon near the Columbia River, Stanfield Secondary School serves about 250 students in grades 7–12. A small agricultural community, Stanfield students have traditionally completed school and gone to work on nearby farms or in agricultural processing plants.

Six years ago Steve Ellis became principal and recognized the need to strengthen the school's academic program. The economy was stagnant. Fewer jobs were available in local businesses, and even agricultural firms wanted employees with some post-secondary education. State funding for education was declining.

The Stanfield community, a small rural town, while supportive of education, was unable to provide additional local resources for this initiative. Steve knew that in order to transform his school he needed to build support among local leaders, employers, and families.

Steve contacted local civic groups in Stanfield and nearby Hermiston and asked to speak with them. He shared his vision for Stanfield and asked for their support. Modest donations helped provide books for the book study and to support students who chose to make visits to Oregon university campuses.

Perhaps most importantly, Steve was a vocal advocate for his vision for Stanfield Secondary School. He talked about his students, he shared their dreams and their successes, and he consistently used every opportunity, formal or informal, to talk about how Stanfield Secondary was preparing students for success in the "new" Oregon economy.

A multi-step approach was used. Steve and his staff talked with local businesses about what they looked for in employees. Armed with these data, they began to talk with each other about what that meant for a small school with limited resources.

Stanfield applied for an Oregon GEAR UP grant, a federal program designed to promote college readiness among under-represented populations. While some students at Stanfield had gone to college, it had not been an emphasis. In the five years prior to 2008 Stanfield had only 8 of its 146 graduates attend one of Oregon's state universities. Recently all but four of the graduating class attended a four-year or community college or a trade school.

Steve and his staff redesigned their professional learning. Rather than occasionally sending members to conferences, they chose to use a book study model. Books about improving instruction, increasing rigor, and engagement were selected, read, and discussed. Every staff member was a member of a small learning group, and the book discussions replaced traditional staff meetings. Through their shared learning they began to redesign classes so that students had a more rigorous academic experience.

Steve described his approach as "finding anyone who would listen" and then "sharing our story." He also said, "Schools can't operate in isolation. We're not preparing students for some generic future. We must build connections to our community and let them know we're committed to assuring our students will be successful not only in high school but beyond."

Additional information about Stanfield Secondary School can be obtained at www.stanfield.k12.or.us.

Collaboration Skills

The Glen Ellyn (IL) School District, a suburban district near Chicago, needed to redesign their middle grades program at Hadley Junior High School, a 6–8 grade school of about 1,200 students.

The district was caught in the maelstrom of stable resources, the need to be more efficient and reduce costs, and increased expectations for student success.

Math teachers desired more instructional time to fully implement a new curriculum. Reading and language arts teachers wanted long instructional blocks taught by a single teacher rather than students having two separate classes. The exploratory classes were dated and modeled after classes in the 1960s.

To address the issues the district launched *Hadley New Horizons,* a planning team that included teachers, administrators, and parents. They were to examine the issues and recommend program modifications.

One absolute parameter given the planning team was that there would be no additional resources provided for the program without persuasive rationale. The team was encouraged to consider the reallocation of resources from one function to another, even abandoning some programs and activities if appropriate.

Central to the adopted plan was re-conceptualizing the structure of the school day. After hearing from every content area and learning about their needs, the planning team recommended reorganizing the day into 15-minute scheduling blocks (27 in all) while not lengthening the school day. The 15-minute increments were chosen to provide flexibility in scheduling the various parts of the school day.

Content areas received varied instructional minutes based on their needs. Language Arts became a 90-minute uninterrupted block. Mathematics classes increased to 60 minutes, while Science and Social Studies classes remained at 45 minutes. Physical Education and Exploratory classes were also 45 minutes and lunch was 30 minutes.

There are few times during the day when the entire student body is passing between classes. That has minimized noise and made the hallways far less hectic. Lunches begin every 15 minutes during the middle of the day, reducing congestion and noise in the lunchroom.

The exploratory program changed dramatically. Students now choose courses based upon their interests. Choices include traditional areas like performing music, performing arts, and fine arts, but now there are options in technology, current events, and application of learning in core subjects. Those classes change from year to year based on interest and need. Every student has daily physical education, a requirement in Illinois.

Overall, the plan increased instructional time in core subjects, provided students with greater choice in exploratory courses, and constrained costs. Perhaps most importantly, the plan was implemented with broad staff and parent support because of the commitment to a collaborative planning model.

Additional information about the Hadley New Horizons program can be found at www.d41.dupage.k12.il.us/schools/hadley/hnh.htm or at the home page of the Hadley website www.d41.dupage.k12.il.us/schools/hadley/.

Final Thoughts

Every principal we meet talks about the challenging economic times. They are expected to do more but to do it with fewer resources. What's important to recognize is that, despite the challenges, it is possible to strengthen and enhance a school's program. It requires committed, visionary leadership, leadership that sees the challenges as an opportunity rather than barrier.

Resources

Tools to Advocate for Your School

www.principals.org/tabid/3788/default.aspx?topic=Tools_to_Advocate_for_Your_School

Holding a Shared Vision—Michigan Department of Education

www.michigan.gov/documents/mde/2-1_383730_7.pdf

Shared Vision—Costa & Kallick (ASCD)

www.ascd.org/publications/books/195188/chapters/Shared-Vision.aspx

The Learning-Centered Principal—R. DuFour

www.ascd.org/publications/educational_leadership/may02/vol59/num08/The_Learning-Centered_Principal.aspx

Strategies for Prospering in the New Normal Environment

The Four *R*'s

Sometimes it's difficult to imagine how schools can survive in the New Normal environment, let alone prosper in these challenging times. However, many schools have not only faced the challenges directly, and effectively, they have also improved, flourished, and prospered. To do so requires the kind of leadership described in Part II of this book, a large measure of creativity, and a hefty dose of courage and conviction.

Part III of this book lays out some of the strategies that effective leaders have used to reduce the budget, refine their operations, reprioritize the school's agenda, and regenerate lost resources—the Four *R*'s that shape the rest of this book. Each chapter explores a different set of strategies and, because we learn best from our colleagues, all of them contain numerous examples of how other school leaders have met the challenges they have faced in their own school settings.

5 | Reduce the Budget

Reducing the budget is one of the most common and unpleasant tasks facing school leaders, but it's also the most essential. This has always been part of school leadership in the normal cycle of plenty and scarcity, but in the New Normal environment "doing more with less" has taken on a virtue of its own. In fact, in some schools, budget-cutting builds such powerful momentum that it becomes a goal in its own right, one that is not necessarily related to either necessary savings or improved operations—simply a leaner budget. We will address these very special circumstances later in this chapter, but, for now, we focus on the essential processes that allow school leaders to make good decisions with the least possible disruption and damage to the school programs.

By now, the low-hanging fiscal fruit is gone, so in most schools or districts it's very difficult to find a way to achieve further budget reductions without affecting something that really matters to someone in the school. The toughest part of the job, according to David Maddox (1999), is reducing the budget without compromising the organization's mission, an increasingly challenging task in an environment where the "fat" has been gone for years and fundamental school operations are being affected by additional cuts.

But even this most unpleasant task, a product of the financial realities of the current environment, can be achieved in ways that minimize damage to the school's central mission, and may, in fact, even produce better outcomes for students, teachers, and staff.

Major elements of an effective budget cutting strategy include careful planning, impact mitigation, effective communication, and focus on hard questions to achieve results.

How Much Money?

Typically, budget cuts are either mandated—as in the case of most government cuts—or result from some kind of fiscal analysis undertaken by a district that projects revenue and expenses in order to identify the size of a financial shortfall.

A careful analysis may also yield information about other factors at work in the school or district that may result in even greater shortfalls or increased revenue potential if they come to fruition. Such an analysis, even in the face of mandated cuts, can be especially helpful in order to identify some of these potential trends:

Changes in enrollment or potential enrollment can occur because of changes in the birth cohort or housing demographics in the district, including changes in the nature of the population being served. Government subsidies are also different for different categories of students—exceptional child education, English language learners, children who live in poverty, or children of military personnel—so a change in one of these populations will have a profound effect on district revenue.

Increased competition from other providers, such as charters, private schools, virtual schools, or home-schooling, can change the demand for school services even if the overall student population demographics don't change.

Unusual cost events, such as a spike in the cost of essential goods or services used by the school. For example, in recent years, increases in fuel costs have required that districts curtail bus transportation routes, divert money from other operating budgets to pay for fuel, and eliminate special transportation options, such as field trips, in order to cover basic transportation needs. Similar increases have occurred in insurance rates, employee medical costs, and security requirements.

More Considerations

In addition to being concerned about the amount of the budget cut, Margaret Barr and George McClellan (2011) write that three factors drive much of the budget-cutting process: (1) time, (2) information, and (3) risk tolerance. Although their excellent book is written for higher education, the principles they advocate are also relevant for districts and individual schools as well.

How Much Time?

How much time is available to achieve the budget savings? If they must be taken in the current year, the approaches are much different, and usually more painful, than a plan that can be implemented over a couple of years.

Some schools try to protect themselves from surprise budget measures by creating budget scenarios that anticipate different conditions and how the school might respond to them. For example, an Ohio district conducted an annual 2/5/10 review, in which every unit was asked to identify how it would respond to a 2% increase, or a 5% or 10% reduction. During that particular fiscal period in the state, the 2% exercise proved to be the least helpful part of the activity, although it did force the schools to consider where they would "invest" future revenue if it became available.

After each budget unit prepared their responses, the principal convened the school's leadership team for a "consequence analysis" of the different scenarios in an effort to ensure that the anticipated budget reductions were not considered in isolation. This prevented proposed reductions in one unit from having an unanticipated effect on another unit. In one particular instance, a change in offerings in the math department had a profound effect on the music program, since a large number of students in advanced mathematics also participated in music ensembles.

At the district level, principals met with the superintendent to discuss how budget cuts in one building might affect other schools, thereby avoiding some potential disasters. The areas typically most affected by these district-level decisions often involve such basics as school stop-start schedules, transportation, teacher assignment, equalized curriculum offerings across schools, and extra-curricular activities. These are among the most "public" decisions a school district can make, so it is critical that both school leaders and board members be congruent in the messages they present to the community.

How Good Is the Information?

The single most important tool for school leaders in making budget reductions is information—good information, and lots of it. Unit leaders need to be held to a very high standard in providing information that will have a potentially profound effect on people, programs, and the entire school community. After all, that information will not only drive the budget-reduction decisions but it will be used to explain those decisions to the people most affected by the cuts—staff, students, parents, and the community.

Anyone with budget responsibilities should be expected to provide complete, documentable information to inform the debate about budget cuts. If budgets are based on projected enrollments, those projections should be documented with evidence rather than being an arm-chair listing of "what we've always done." And this evidence should be as refined as possible in order to make the best possible decisions. For example, the number of students currently enrolled in Algebra 2 and Trigonometry may not be sufficient to project enrollments in Calculus. A more accurate estimate may rely on the number of students likely to complete Algebra and Trig *successfully* and who plan to take more advanced math to meet specific college admission requirements.

The same principle is true for other, more ephemeral projections. Can the athletic director predict attendance at games? Can the people who run the PTO book fair project how much income the fair might provide for the school library? Are higher-subsidy special education enrollments stable? Is there likely to be an influx of special needs or high-need students because of re-districting? An Illinois principal uses this matrix to encourage his staff to gather good information in support of a school-wide budget analyses.

While it takes some time and effort for department chairs, faculty, team leaders, or other staff with budget responsibilities to complete this exercise, this ensures a thoughtful, evidence-based analysis of the current status and anticipated needs of each part of the school's program. It also makes clear just what kind of information is required to make a case for budget adjustments and discourages some of the peer and political pressures often brought to the process. In fact, the "confidence rating" also requires that staff members conducting the analysis actually rate the amount of confidence they have in their own projections, further eliminating inflated estimates, "the sky is falling" scenarios, and some of the other unproductive strategies that intrude on a rational budget process.

Need	Rationale	Information/ Evidence	Source of Information/ Evidence	Comment	Confidence*
2 sections of Calculus 1	Provide slots for 36 students.	~Students projected to pass Alg2/ Trig. ~Students anticipating need for Calculus 1.	~Midterm Exams in Alg2/Trig. ~Survey of students. ~Consult with Guidance Counselors. ~NCTM Recommended class sizes for Calc1.	May be offset by dual enrollment course from local community college.	4
3 Double Algebra 1 classes for incoming students (6 class sessions)	Provide slots for 75 students needing 2 periods of Alg 1 per day.	~Incoming ninth graders with low math scores on state assessment. ~Number of 9th graders not completing district proficiency exams in Alg 1.	~State test data from eighth grade class, feeder middle schools. ~Mid-term results on course proficiency tests in Algebra 1.	Both tests required for graduation.	5

*Confidence in estimate: 5 = very high; 4 = high; 3 = uncertain; 2 = low; 1 = very low; 0 = none

How Much Risk Can We Tolerate?

This is one of the toughest decisions school leaders must make because it deals with two critical elements in any budget reduction strategy:

If we gamble on a decision, what happens if it doesn't work?

How much stress will the strategy put on morale that may already be pretty fragile?

Further, there are multiple personalities that need to be considered in assessing risk: individual leaders, such as principals, superintendents, staff members, union leaders, students and parents; and groups, such as school boards or other policy and governing bodies that not only have individual risk tolerance levels for each member, but "official" risk tolerance levels that may be affected by law and policy, political forces, their advisors, or public opinion.

In a southern California district, anticipated revenue shortfalls were met with a large investment in integrated course-management technology that included paperless communication and class materials, student/teacher/parent communication systems, telephone and text-messaging replacements, networked course access that allowed for virtual learning, and even electronic textbooks and other course material. This system replaced dozens of individual expenditures: textbook and instructional materials acquisition, leasing and staffing of duplicating equipment, an existing telephone notification system for parents, and even some instructional positions because savings could be achieved through online instruction. Savings were especially significant in low-demand courses (such as a fifth year of a foreign language) where virtual instruction allowed the school to access university online courses for their students.

The risk for this decision was substantial. Jobs were affected, even lost, and in some cases the very nature of instruction was altered considerably. The potential for a catastrophic collapse of morale was high, and the likelihood of community backlash was unknowable. It required that school and district staff learn new ways of doing things, and long-standing contracts be renegotiated. Why on earth would any rational school leader take such a risk?

In this case, school leaders did their homework—a lot of it. And they consulted broadly with people most likely to be affected: teachers, union representatives, board members, parents, students, and leaders in the broader community. The purpose of these consultations wasn't to build support for the new initiatives—not yet, anyway—but to find out the kinds of concerns, issues, and potential objections that existed among the district's constituents. In short, they did a broad-based risk assessment.

For the most part, these consultations were held with job-alike groups so that district leaders could understand issues unique to each constituent group. Also, that prevented conflicting points of view from being staked out early in the process and making later compromises more difficult. At each meeting, district leaders sought the following kinds of information, although the conversations were as informal as possible, and the matrix below was used to summarize information from the meetings.

Component of Proposal	Potential Effect(s)	Possible Mitigation of Effect(s)	Notes and Comments
Which parts of the proposed move to a greatly enriched technological learning management platform will have an effect on members of this group?	What will be the effect, positive and negative, of each part of this new initiative on members of this group? What are the "deal-breakers"?	How might these negative effects be mitigated and the positive effects enhanced?	Are there any special consider-ations that need to be included in the plan-ning of this new initiative?

After conducting their risk assessment, the California district proceeded with the plan, with a number of modifications, including these:

● They relied on naturally occurring vacancies rather than lay-offs to achieve personnel cuts. Employees whose positions were eliminated were offered the opportunity to retrain for another position or accept a severance package.

● Teachers were given first opportunities to teach out-of-certification courses if they agreed to earn necessary certifications within a given time period.

● Community volunteers in this high-tech region were used to provide professional development for district staff to learn new technologies already in common use in area businesses.

● Ample training was provided for everyone, and coaches were made available "on demand" to help staff adjust to the new technologies.

Why It Worked

Was this a perfect solution? No. There were some very unhappy people. Some left; others stayed and, eventually, complied with the new directions.

Did it work? Eventually. It took effort, training, support, and modeling by respected peers.

Did it achieve the necessary budget savings? Not right away, but over the course of a couple of years, as people became comfortable with the new technology and retirements and relocations produced natural personnel savings, the district exceeded its budget reduction targets considerably.

But four key features of this initiative actually made the project work:

Good data and information. The district was very careful to get good, honest information about the cost of the new innovations and the actual savings that could be realized.

Trust. Trust in the district administration and board was generally high because they had been forthright and transparent in earlier budget planning. People were pretty sure that both the extent of the crisis and the proposed savings from the new initiative were real.

An open process. Starting with good data, and continuing with a solid risk assessment, the district could roll out a budget cutting plan that contained few surprises and as many accommodations as possible to various constituent groups.

An understanding of community context. This was a technologically sophisticated community where many people worked in high-tech industries. Many of the innovations being proposed were common practices in parents' workplaces. Indeed, most parents were impressed to see the district move into the 21st century!

Budget-Cutting Strategies and Approaches

For something that has been going on in schools for as long as budget cutting, there isn't much variation in the strategies that school leaders use to achieve savings. Most of the approaches include some combination of the following strategies.

Budget Freeze

Although not really a budget-cutting approach, a freeze can save money over the short term. More importantly, it signals to staff that things are serious, and that money is tight. A freeze usually means that discretionary spending is either halted completely or conducted with high-level scrutiny. Travel, equipment purchases, and other expenditures not directly related to core program operations may be halted, and hiring of non-essential personnel may be curtailed or eliminated. A freeze is often used as an interim step while the school or district considers other ways of achieving longer-term budget reductions.

Across-the-Board Cuts

One of the first decisions that leaders facing a budget cut must make is whether the cuts should be across the board or targeted. Typically, in an across-the-board cut, budget directors are instructed to reduce their budget by a specific percentage by a specific date.

Across-the-board cuts are relatively easy to administer and give at least the appearance of fairness: everyone shares the pain. It also empowers other administrators (department chairs, athletic directors, team leaders) to participate in the process by identifying where they can take their share of the cut and do the least damage to their operations. Sometimes, across-the-board cuts are refined slightly so that specific units, such as academic departments, administration, support services, etc., are required to take a larger or smaller cut. In this scenario, administrative units often take the hardest hit to show that the administration is doing its part to reduce expenditures. In some cases, administrative cuts are combined with salary freezes to achieve further reductions, largely because administrative salaries are not generally governed by a collective bargaining agreement.

The downsides of across-the-board cuts are many because they are indiscriminate and may not account for any unit's ability to absorb a cut. If earlier cuts had been absorbed in a specific area, such as the administration losing an assistant principal or attendance clerk, an additional cut may actually damage core functions and have repercussions across the school or district.

Further, accountability standards and state mandates may greatly reduce a specific unit's ability to take their "fair share" of an across-the-board cut. Is a cut in the math department, for example, more significant to the school's overall performance than one in a less accountability-critical area? Such effects may, again, have major effects on a school's overall standing and reputation.

Targeted Reductions

Targeted cuts can be directed by top-level leaders or rely on more partici-pation by other administrators. Typically, targeted cuts take one of several forms: looking for excess funding that is no longer necessary for main-taining core programs, ending certain services or cutting back on support services, or program elimination and reduction. Obviously, participatory measures help garner group buy-in, but, frankly, may require more good will than a leader can muster, and may introduce competition and ran-cor that will ultimately do more damage to the organization than the cuts themselves.

Targeted reductions rely on the premise that certain functions are more central to the mission of the school and, therefore, should be protected as much as possible. In this scenario, funds from specific budget lines—such as professional development, instructional materials, equipment, or supplies—may be called back to the central office to cover shortfalls. Unfortunately, by now, most of the easy cuts have been made, so there are very few options available that do not directly affect school programs.

Restructuring

More dramatic than a freeze or cuts (across the board or targeted), restruc-turing involves major changes in the school and its operations. This may involve combining programs and administrative processes, or consolidating operations in significant ways (Valenti, 2009).

Restructuring is generally a very painful and difficult process. Because it involves people and the way they do their jobs, it is loaded with emo-tion and, sometimes, organized resistance. Combining art and music into an "Arts" department brings up huge personnel questions—such as "Who will chair this new unit?" or "Who will stay and who will go?" Organizational issues prevail as well: Whose events will get the most support? How will "boosters" be included? Most important, what is gained and what is lost through any restructuring move? And will savings offset organizational and political costs?

The issue of restructuring is sufficiently complex that we will explore it in some detail in Chapters 6 and 7.

Program Elimination

Eliminating programs is the most dramatic and difficult of all budget-cutting measures, especially if it's a "legacy" program that has numerous loyal alumni and strong support in the community. Ironically, it is often the most effective and most efficient way to achieve a budget reduction while still preserving the integrity of the school's core mission. But priorities change, and so do the interests and needs of students currently enrolled. So the task of school leaders who seek to eliminate a program is three-fold:

● Connect the decision to new priorities and new needs.

● Eliminate the program gradually, preserving some of its important elements.

● Demonstrate compassion and sensitivity to those who have an investment in the program.

The elimination of a Home Economics program by a Florida high school provides an outstanding example of just how all of these factors work together to produce a good decision.

Compassionate Budget Cutting

A principal whose staff included one of the longest-serving and most popular home economics teachers in the county needed to eliminate that program in order to bolster support for a growing medical technology program. He started by sharing enrollment data with the home economics teacher and asking her to help him think about how elements of the curriculum might be plugged into other academies operating in the school. Together, they developed a number of options focused on the teacher's special interest: foods and nutrition. She developed a module for the child care technology program on child nutrition; offered a similar module in the health sciences academy; and actually worked with the horticulture teacher to include food gardening and community nutrition in his program. Keeping in mind the home economics teacher's impending retirement, the principal found modest resources, mostly in the form of student assistance, to place the modules on a technological platform so that they could be offered after she left the district. When the program ended, he also recovered needed instructional space, and even picked up some funds by selling off the home economics lab equipment—appliances, kitchen fixtures, cabinets and shelving. This principal solved a problem by getting the home economics teacher engaged in the process so that when the cuts were announced she was on board. Most important, in addition to saving money, he demonstrated compassion in making tough decisions.

What Are the Elements of a Good Decision? Good fiscal decision making has several key elements:

High-Quality Information helps everyone understand the deficits, the steps taken to soften their effect, and the data used to make budget decisions. Not everyone will be happy with the outcome, but the process itself needs to be as transparent as possible.

Consistency of the Messages. People rely on those they trust (including social media "friends") for information and not necessarily the school or district. Invest in "internal public relations" so that everyone in the school is giving essentially the same message about the cuts.

Confidentiality. Everyone knows of a nightmare story of how a leaked e-mail has derailed months of planning and leadership effort. The key to success? Be careful of what you say and to whom you say it!

Trust Levels in the Organization. If school staff are aligned around a common vision of the organization's mission and its situation, they are more likely to convey a consistent message about the reductions and the need for them.

Address Key Issues Directly. Address real concerns as soon as possible.

Everyone is looking for the answer to one question—"will I lose my job, or will it be changed in some way?" Every message about the cuts will be screened for clues that may or may not be accurate, and are almost certain to be anxiety-provoking.

Making Promises. If possible, don't make them. People have long memories, so a statement made early in the process may restrict future actions or force leaders to abandon earlier commitments—exacerbating the negative effect on morale and trust.

Dissent. Dissenting opinions aren't always comfortable to hear, but they are important for two very critical reasons: they may show an aspect of the problem or the budget-cutting plan that no one thought of earlier, and, just as important, they may telegraph the kinds of arguments and resistance school leaders will get when they roll out the budget plan.

Different Audiences. In making announced cuts, be absolutely truthful and consistent in the messages that are sent out, but also recognize that different groups want different information. Students may want to know if cuts affect their favorite classes, teachers, or college admission opportunities. Parents will be concerned about the loss of academic programs, school safety, transportation, and schedules. The larger community may be concerned about the effect of cuts on the school's image and that of the community itself. Teachers are concerned about jobs, assignments, and their most treasured curriculum areas. It may be helpful to invest in some public relations assistance in structuring appropriate messages for each group.

Someone Will Be Unhappy. Leaders can't control individual interpretations of events. Budget cuts are tough, and despite best efforts to behave fairly, someone is going to be angry about the outcome. Leaders accept that and move on.

The Bottom Line

Budget cuts aren't easy, and nothing can make them so. But they can be achieved with a minimum of rancor and still preserve the integrity and mission of the organization. When the cuts become so frequent and so severe that the school's mission is jeopardized, more thoughtful and even dramatic changes may be needed—changes in the fundamental ways that schools do their work. The remainder of this book is devoted to exploring these options for coping with, and even prospering, in the New Normal environment.

Think About It

Take some time to think about your own budget priorities. Answer these basic questions for yourself before launching a discussion among your staff or leadership team. In fact, have the rest of the leadership team answer them as well.

1. Where do you think the "low hanging" fiscal fruit can be found if we face a cut?
2. What should be protected at all costs?
3. Where would we get the most consensus on a budget reduction among staff? Among parents? Among students? In the community? From the district and board?
4. What works best for us—across the board or targeted?
5. What information do we need to make the best possible decisions?

Now Try This

A Message from the Leadership

Try drafting a letter (or bulleted list) for different groups in your school explaining why budget cuts are necessary and what their effects might be on the school. What information, arguments, and assurances could you present to teachers, staff, students, parents, and community members? What will each group be most concerned about? You may never send it, but it will help you think about the concerns of different groups.

Leadership in Action

Check out these resources to see how other school leaders have met some pretty significant fiscal challenges in their own schools.

Duval County (FL) Budget Cutting Planning Sheet. This template shows how one district approached the analysis of budget reduction options. Although designed for district level cuts, this is a useful example for how an individual school might approach the same task.

www.duvalschools.org/static/aboutdcps/departments/budget/down loads/Budget_Reduction.pdf

Budget Reduction Strategies from School Staff, Community. An interesting report from the Pinellas County (FL) Schools shows the result of community-wide conversations about needed budget cuts. Most interesting are the items on which there is at least some agreement. www.pcsb.org/index.php?option=com_content&view=article&id=1357&Ite mid=930

School Budget Hold 'Em. This clever, online game allows school leaders to create different budget scenarios, ranging from 10% cuts to 10% increases, and challenges the "players" to consider consequences and alternative actions. http://erstrategies.org/resources/details/school_budget_holdem/

Breaking Down School Budgets by Margaret Roza. This very interesting article shows how to track dollars into the classroom by determining what it costs to deliver different types of instruction. Roza provides a very unique "granular" analysis of how money is actually spent on instruction. http://educationnext.org/breaking-down-school-budgets-2/

First Person Tale of Cost-Cutting by Nathan Levenson. (You Tube Video: www.youtube.com/watch?v=SAGOicN5Rcw). Levenson's tale of his experience as a superintendent in Massachusetts tracks the approaches, strategies, successes, and failures of major budget realignments and reductions. Through it all, the focus remained on boosting student achievement in the midst of a fiscal crisis. This very challenging presentation is a preview of his equally provocative and inventive book, *Smarter Budgets, Smarter Schools* from Harvard Education Press. http://hepg.org/hep/book/163

6 | Refine School Practices and Stretch the School Dollar

It seems as if schools never have enough money. It's hard to remember a time when schools had all the money they believed that they needed, and when there wasn't a discussion of where cuts needed to be made in an upcoming budget. But now, the reductions from traditional funding sources are real and deep. And they have been going on long enough so that a lot of discretionary money—or even all of it—is gone from school budgets. As one Ohio principal put it in a confidential email to author Howard Johnston, "We cut the remaining fat in 2006; by 2009 we were slicing off the muscle, and now we're cutting away the bone."

The Authors' Challenge . . . and Yours

Between us, we have more than 75 years of experience in education at all levels. We are familiar with the ways schools function, understand the nuances of school operations, and, if not always happy with them, know the reasons for established practices and procedures. We're pretty much like most experienced educators: generally satisfied with our success in the system as it is while accepting, intellectually, the need to change some basic practices.

That made this one of the most difficult chapters to write. We had to read literature that we don't always examine closely and spend a lot of time considering the ideas and actions of people who have been very critical of education, sometimes even of the things that we have done or recommended. We have had to venture into the work of individual authors, think tanks, politicians, pundits, and policy-makers with whom we have disagreed for many years. In the interests of fairness and completeness, we had to open our minds and suspend some long-held beliefs about the way things are and should be. It wasn't easy.

This chapter is about refining school practices, and the first thing we had to refine was our thinking about what's necessary, what's simply customary, and what's best for kids and their learning. Now we are asking you to do the same thing.

This chapter may not be any easier for you to read than it was for us to write. But we hope you will think about the ideas presented here, consider them in the context of the New Normal, and discuss them with your faculty and leadership team. We also hope you will share your own reactions and thoughts about these ideas and how they might be made to work on our blog: http://leadersdoingmorewithless.blogspot.com.

Clearly, as stated elsewhere in this book, we aren't going to tax or cut our way out of this current fiscal situation. We may grow our way out partially, as state revenues increase in an improving economy, but doing more with less—the mantra of the New Normal—is with us for the foreseeable future.

Nathan Levenson, a former Superintendent in Massachusetts and author of *Smarter Budgets, Smarter Schools: How to Survive and Thrive in Tight Times* writes in a Thomas B. Fordham Foundation Policy Brief (December 2012, p. 1),

Though the K–12 finance picture is bleak, it need not paralyze district leadership. Fortunately, strategies are available that can raise achievement and provide a well-rounded education to all children without breaking the bank. But good leaders must distinguish what expenditures really make a difference from a hundred that don't. Education has long suffered from clever ideas that turned out to be anything but. Whole language, classroom technology, and zillions of hours of professional development, for example, haven't delivered on their lofty promises. As budgets tighten, districts will devise all manner of cost-saving strategies—some wise, some foolish, some constructive, some damaging.

He then goes on to explain in some detail three key actions for making what he considers to be good financial decisions:

1. cultivating a new mind-set that prioritizes both achievement and cost-efficiency;
2. making staffing decisions based on student needs rather than adult preferences; and
3. managing special education spending for better outcomes and greater cost-effectiveness (Levenson, 2012, December).

Even without exploring these actions in detail (which Levenson does articulately and succinctly), we can tell that his recommendations are not going to be easy to implement or very popular with many segments of the school and community. And that is the foundation for the key lessons in this chapter:

1. The easy actions have already been taken, some with poor results;
2. There are some strategies that are more difficult, but still can result in both substantial savings and improved learning;
3. The actions that will be necessary if we don't achieve substantial efficiencies now will be much more difficult later.

Michael Petrilli (2012, April) writes about the three premises that should guide all of the actions taken to refine school practices in search of better performance and lower costs:

1. **"Solving our budget crisis shouldn't come at the expense of children**. We should do everything we can to protect students' learning opportunities, improve the effectiveness and productivity of their schools (and other providers), and continue to boost their achievement.
2. **Nor can it come from teachers' sacrifice alone**. Depressing teachers' salaries forever isn't a recipe for recruiting bright young people into education—or retaining the excellent teachers we have.
3. **Quick fixes aren't a good answer; we need fundamental changes that enhance productivity**. The reforms—and

investments—with the greatest payoff are those that will maximize student outcomes at lower cost. And since education is overwhelmingly a people business—and most of the system's costs are in personnel—the most promising reforms are those that rethink our staffing model: whom we hire, how we pay them, and what we do with their time."

Petrilli adds what is going through the mind of every educator at this point: "We are well aware that local officials don't have carte blanche to address budget challenges any way they want. Federal and state regulations, collective-bargaining agreements, and plain old local politics make solving these problems extraordinarily challenging." The remainder of this chapter is devoted to exploring some of these solutions—some of which may be as challenging as the problems they are designed to solve.

What *Doesn't* Work

According to many writers, some of the most commonly used practices to lower school costs may achieve savings in the short run, but they are likely to do damage to both long-term fiscal health and student academic performance (Petrilli, 2012, April).

Shrinking the Workforce by Laying Off the Newest Teachers

Some research has shown that "last hired, first fired policies" may actually lower student achievement significantly, especially if there is an effective beginning teacher mentorship program in place. The effect of this policy tends to be felt more dramatically in high poverty schools because they usually have a disproportionate number of junior faculty. Furthermore, the policy is costly. Not only do younger teachers have lower salaries, but, like Social Security and Medicare, the contributions of younger workers to pension and health insurance programs help fund current benefits. Reducing the number of workers contributing to the system but not yet using it stresses pension plans and drives health premiums higher.

Reducing and Narrowing the Curriculum

Some districts treat art, music, PE, health, or foreign languages as "extras" that can be eliminated without harm. Even social studies and science may be shortchanged in states where they are not part of the state-wide accountability plan. But the real cost of such a bare-bones program is that students are less well-prepared for college entrance or to compete in a knowledge-based global economy. Instead of cutting the programs, schools should seek ways to cut the costs of offering them—strategies for which are offered later in this chapter.

Furloughs Reduce Learning Time and Raise the Cost of Schooling

Shortening the school day, eliminating class days, or closing the school for prolonged periods moves the United States away from the practices in other countries with whom we compete and may actually cost more than it saves. Salary schedules are left intact but teachers actually earn less because they work fewer days. But escalating salaries the next year make it nearly impossible for the district to add back lost days and may even lead to longer furloughs in subsequent years. Even worse, while employees lose salary, benefit costs remain the same, so the cost per day of instruction is actually higher. All of this reduces learning time and leads to financial hardships for employees.

Passing Costs on to Students and Families

Charging parents for art, music, sports, Advanced Placement exams, and other "extras" widens the gap between the haves and have-nots and raises fundamental questions about the nature of public schooling. Beyond the difficulty of coming up with the money to pay these fees, some parents may not see the value of art, music, or AP classes, so their children are deprived of opportunities because of parental decisions that may be quite uninformed.

Now Comes the Hard Part

If easy things don't work very well, that means the things that might work must be harder to do. Unfortunately, individual school leaders have relatively little discretion over some of the major costs of school operations. Salary schedules, transportation costs, insurance, benefits, and other expenses that make up the bulk of the school's budget are typically decided at the district level or may even be mandated by state or federal law. The good news is that there are still a number of actions that principals can take that will help save money and continue to deliver high-quality service to students, even it looks different from the way we have always done it. The biggest challenge—the hard part—is to open our experienced minds to new ways of thinking about delivering educational services. To help do just that, the remainder of this chapter is devoted to strategies actually used in schools to refine their practices and lower their costs.

Even difficult tasks can be made more manageable by thinking about them systematically. Fortunately, the Annenberg Institute for School Reform provides a helpful guide for planning and implementing some of these difficult refinements (Barnes, 2004).

There are four areas over which individual school leaders have varying degrees of control, at least in their buildings:

1. Human Resource Use and Development
2. School Organization
3. Fiscal and Technical Resources
4. Social Resources

Also, as some of our examples illustrate, individual schools may get permission to try innovative refinements or even become a pilot for a district-wide initiative.

Human Resource Use and Development

According to Jim Collins in *Good to Great*, one of the most important considerations for leaders is to make sure the right people are "on the bus." If a leader already has a bus full of people with little chance to change that mix, he or she needs to focus on three key issues:

- The skills of the staff
- Staff knowledge about effective practice
- How staff are used for maximum performance at the lowest cost

Michael Petrilli suggests that there are several general strategies for refining the human resource mix in schools that can be influenced by individual school leaders. Some can be implemented only at the district or state level, but others can result in significant savings at the school level. The key strategy, according to Petrilli (2012, April), is to **Aim for a leaner, more productive, better paid workforce in the school.**

Education is a "people-intensive business" so it's almost impossible to reduce costs without letting people go. In the past two decades, largely as a result of federal and state initiatives, schools have hired numerous program administrators, aides, assistants, support staff, IT people, and other specialists. Petrilli believes that schools should redefine these roles, and those of teachers, for increased productivity and pay for professional staff.

- **Ask teachers to take on additional responsibilities for additional pay**. Can they do without an aide? Take on a larger student load? Help with quasi-administrative tasks such as student supervision in cafeterias or other unstructured settings? Coordinate AP testing or the IB program or run an after-school or extended summer program? If so, they can realize significant salary improvements at the same time that the school saves the additional costs, such as benefits, of an additional position.

- **Reduce ancillary positions.** Can the district do with fewer specialists, coordinators, aides, or other specialized personnel? Can teachers take over some of these tasks for extra compensation? Is it possible for two schools to share positions that have some flexibility—such as a librarian, art teacher, or counselors? Two neighboring districts in rural Oregon actually share two teachers; one district hired a foreign language teacher and the other hired an advanced math teacher, and these teachers divide their time between the two district high schools. Because the cost of employee benefits can be quite high (30%–40% of salary costs in some locations), reducing employee "head count" helps contain a significant expense, even if additional money is invested in boosting salaries for additional work or teaching in unique circumstances.

- **Trade down** (Levenson, 2012). Too often, art gets cut to save reading, or nurses and counselors are cut to save math and English. "Trading down" implies that the school can provide similar services at lower cost. (It's sort of like giving up the new SUV with its high monthly payments in favor of a used economy car in order to save money for a down payment on a house or pay for college.) Levenson says, "Sure, some of these alternatives aren't as good as the original, but they are better than nothing at all. If districts move less-critical functions to less-skilled staff, and then supplement with careful hiring, good supervision, and high-quality professional development, they can still serve students well at much lower cost." He then provides some interesting examples currently in use.

○ In one district, 14 social work graduate students were recruited as interns to provide basic services in the schools. They were supervised and coached each week by an experienced, certified counselor, but were able to handle a lot of the routine cases and freed up other professional staff to handle more complex matters.

○ A district in a high-tech region replaced Instructional Technology support staff with tech-savvy parents working part time or as volunteers. In other schools, students fill the role of IT support in a service learning or work-study arrangement.

○ When a Florida middle school lost a custodian, the staff decided to forego replacing the position and created voluntary homeroom teams that rotated taking care of some basic, daily building cleanup. A full-time custodian handled major tasks involving chemicals and machinery, but routine work was performed by student teams. Weekend work parties involved students, parents, alumni, and other community members in helping to landscape the grounds and perform minor maintenance, like painting and decorating the building.

● **Invest in building staff capacity.** Staff members are certainly not interchangeable, but people can learn new skills that prepare them to take on more responsibilities and perform roles lost to budget cuts. Rather than "one size fits all" staff development, many schools are now using their meager resources to retrain existing, perhaps underutilized, staff for high-demand roles that they cannot afford to fill. Others are training staff to fill ancillary roles, such as Instructional Technology support or library paraprofessional, in order to keep service levels high and costs low.

○ In one outstanding example, a Texas high school retrained one of its secretaries to replace an IT support person who had retired. This individual spent several hours a day in the administrative support role, and the remainder of the time providing IT services. In addition, she coordinated a team of student "techs" who helped teachers and students troubleshoot technology problems.

○ In Utah, instructional aides were trained to staff a computer lab in which students worked independently on distance-learning courses in advanced subjects offered by a state university. All of the instruction was individualized, and academic support was provided online, so the aide was responsible for the management of the lab and for offering technology assistance when needed.

School Organization

The most obvious artifact of school organization is the schedule. It tells us how people spend their time, how much time is allocated for different kinds of activities, and with whom people spend their day. On another level, it's a very clear statement of the school's values. Are all subjects held in equal esteem? Do all teachers have similar workloads? Does the schedule segregate students by ability, ethnicity, economic status, or some other less obvious criterion? Do students have equal access to educational opportunities?

For the purposes of this book, it is helpful to look at school systems and structures as a way of determining if the school is spending its resources on the things that it, the community, and the state accountability system claim are important. In other words, given limited resources, are we using them to get the most achievement bang for our buck? Two organizational features of the school are clearly open to refinement by leaders: class size and time.

Class Size enjoys a special place in the hearts and minds of educators, parents, and most school leaders. Unfortunately, the research doesn't necessarily support what most of us believe—that small class size is linked to increased student performance. In fact, most research (Whitehurst & Chingos, 2011) indicates that only relatively large reductions in class size—about 7 students or 32%—result in achievement gains, and those are most pronounced in very early grades and among the most impoverished students.

Still, almost no one believes that research, so most school districts will do almost anything—cut anything—in order to preserve smaller class sizes. Indeed, the Florida Constitution was amended by voters in 2002 to set absolute class size limits in core classes in the state's schools. Since then, the Legislature has appropriated nearly $25 billion for operational and facilities expenses associated with the amendment. In Florida's fiscal environment, that money had to come from somewhere—and many believe that it resulted in large cuts in other school resources.

Often those cuts involve programs and practices that have a stronger research evidence base than the one that exists for class size. As Levenson (2012) writes, "Smaller class sizes may indeed be preferable, but at what cost? Supplemental reading programs, effective professional development, curriculum leadership, and the use of student data to drive instruction all have greater impacts on student learning and are relatively inexpensive compared to maintaining small classes. Despite their proven importance, however, these services are often cut, and cut deeply, during a downturn."

The bottom line? Keeping class size from rising by one or two students is probably not worth giving up other, cost-effective programs, with the possible exception of early grades and among impoverished students. New technologies and professional development focused explicitly on managing larger groups of students can help to sustain, or even improve, achievement in slightly larger classes. As with most interventions, though, class size may not be a case of "one size fits all." Some teachers may be better prepared to handle more students, with additional compensation or some other incentives, and specific subjects may be more amenable to larger classes than others.

Time utilization is one of the school leader's most powerful tools in managing both costs and school performance.

Scheduling expert Ron Williamson (1998) advises that principals not view the schedule as just an organizational necessity, but as a resource—just like money—to be managed, leveraged, and invested. Time, then, becomes a powerful tool for refining school practices to improve performance and lower costs.

According to Williamson (2008, March), scheduling priorities vary based on goals. If the goal is longer instructional blocks so that teachers can use an array of instructional strategies, then that becomes the priority. If the goal is time to schedule participation in extension/remediation activities, then that becomes the priority. If the goal is to lower costs, the schedule can help achieve that as well.

The best schedules are developed based on data about student performance, student learning needs, available resources, and curricular and instructional requirements. The schedule becomes a tool that teachers can use to address the learning needs of students and to provide a rich, engaging educational experience.

One of the most powerful instructional tools is the use of longer, more flexible instructional blocks. Variations of block schedules have become the common scheduling model in many schools at all levels.

Scheduling Alternatives

There are four ways to provide instructional flexibility (Williamson, 1998). They vary dramatically from the traditional fixed-period schedule that is organized around curricular departments where all classes are of equal length. Most fixed-period schedules minimize instructional flexibility, and there is little opportunity for shared or collaborative planning. It can also be expensive.

The other approaches provide greater flexibility. They include various forms of (1) block schedules, (2) alternating day schedules, (3) rotating schedules, and (4) dropped schedules. The model a school chooses should be based on a thorough analysis of the advantages and disadvantages of each and should be aligned with school goals and cost-benefits. Some schedules allow for sharing teachers across departments or schools, some don't. Some are better designed to accommodate both low-enrollment and high-enrollment classes. It is important for principals to consider both the academic purpose *and* the potential costs of each model.

Longer instructional periods, called blocks, are created in a block schedule. Alternating schedules vary the schedule from day-to-day, commonly alternating days. The other two models include a rotating schedule that rotates the placement of classes from day-to-day. In this model, a class may meet at different times every day of the week. The fourth approach is a dropped schedule where one class is dropped so that other activities may occur. In one school, for example, two periods a week were dropped so that student clubs could meet. The classes that were dropped vary from week to week, minimizing the impact on an individual class.

Block Schedule

A block schedule is characterized by longer instructional periods. In schools organized into teacher teams, the teams may teach a common schedule and may vary the length of classes they teach. In the example below, the team has a longer block of instructional time in the morning and afternoon. The team decides how to distribute the time among core classes.

Sample Teams Schedule

Mon	Tues	Wed	Thu	Fri
Core	Core	Core	Core	Core
Expl.	Expl.	Expl.	Expl.	Expl.
Expl.	Expl.	Expl.	Expl.	Expl.
Core	Core	Core	Core	Core

Longer instructional blocks provide teachers greater control over the selection of instructional strategies. Rather than being constrained by the limitations of a fixed period, teachers can select instructional practices that match the learning needs of their students. Blocks also allow teachers to "cover" for each other, often eliminating the need for substitutes.

Longer instructional blocks can also often positively impact school climate. Because there may be fewer class changes, there are fewer disciplinary referrals. When the block schedule includes fewer classes each day, it often reduces stress for both students and teachers.

A common misconception is that a block schedule must include long blocks every day of the week. In order to have each class meet several times each week, block schedules are often mixed with fixed-period schedules. The following example shows how longer blocks can be mixed with shorter class periods. In this school, the goal was to ensure that every class met four times each week.

Mon	Tues	Wed	Thu	Fri
1	1	1	4	1
2		2		2
3	2	3	5	3
4		4		4
5	3	5	6	5
6		6		6

Monday, Wednesday, and Friday provide 50-minute class periods with each class meeting once. Tuesday and Thursday are used for 105-minute class periods with only three classes meeting each day.

Alternating Schedule

An alternating schedule, often called an "A" and "B" schedule, includes classes that alternate from day to day. A version of the block schedule, the alternating schedule generally provides longer instructional periods every day.

Mon	Tues	Wed	Thu	Fri
1	5	1	5	1
2	6	2	6	2
3	7	3	7	3
4	8	4	8	4

The schedule continues to alternate every day throughout the semester or year. In the example above, for the following week, classes 5, 6, 7, and 8 would meet on Monday, Wednesday, and Friday while classes 1, 2, 3, and 4 would meet on Tuesday and Thursday.

Rotating Schedules

A schedule that rotates changes the order of classes from day to day. When a rotating schedule is used, teachers and students report that the schedule changes their perception of one another and of the content area, often because both students and teachers perform differently at different times of the day. For example, in a traditional schedule, a class might always meet just before lunch, but in a rotating schedule the meeting time would rotate throughout the day.

Mon	Tues	Wed	Thu	Fri
1	2	3	4	5
2	3	4	5	6
3	4	5	6	1
4	5	6	1	2
5	6	1	2	3
6	1	2	3	4

By itself, a rotating schedule does not provide longer instructional blocks, but when rotation is paired with other approaches, it can result in some schedule designs that support longer instructional blocks.

A team with two long instructional blocks might find those blocks scheduled at different times each day of the week, providing greater instructional flexibility.

Mon	Tues	Wed	Thu	Fri
1	2	3	4	5
2	3	4	5	6
3	4	5	6	1
4	5	6	1	2
5	6	1	2	3
6	1	2	3	4

Dropped Schedule

A dropped schedule is one where something drops out of the schedule so that something else can be added. In many schools, an advisory, activity, enrichment, or remediation period is often added.

In one southeastern Michigan school, the student schedule included seven classes but only six met on any day for 60-minute periods. The classes rotated throughout the week, each meeting four times. This created two long instructional periods that were scheduled for intervention classes, large group student activities, and seminar activities with individual teachers. These periods were also used for teachers to meet for professional development and common planning. Some weeks, the teacher groups met by content area, and other weeks the meetings were interdisciplinary.

Mon	Tues	Wed	Thu	Fri
1	7	5	4	2
2	Seminar	6	5	3
3	1	7	6	4
4	2	1	Seminar	5
5	3	2	7	6
6	4	3	1	7

Four goals guided the development of the dropped schedule: (1) To have longer classes—60 minutes instead of 45 minutes, (2) To provide an opportunity for intervention classes for students, (3) To make time for teachers to meet, work collaboratively, and participate in professional development, and (4) To allow every class to meet as frequently as possible.

Providing flexibility in the schedule facilitates an instructionally rich program and may help to contain costs. Such a schedule must be complemented by other allotments including time for teachers to work collaboratively and to participate in professional development focused on student achievement.

Fiscal and Technical Resources

Although the central issue in dealing with the New Normal is lack of financial resources, two key strategies for refining school operations involve looking carefully at how resources are used and re-allocating them within existing constraints.

1. Spend money on what works (and stop spending it on things that don't).
2. Integrate technology thoughtfully.

Spend Money on What Works. Just about anyone in the school can identify things that work and things that don't. The problem is how to have that discussion in a way that puts everything on the table and, to the extent possible, reduces the influence of narrow self-interests. One way to have a productive discussion is with the "Stop, Start, Continue" activity described at the end of this chapter.

The activity itself is simple. Just ask your school leaders (both your formal leadership team and the informal leaders in the building) to make three lists:

1. Things we should STOP doing (and spending money on), and why.
2. Things we should START doing, and why.
3. Things we should CONTINUE doing, or do more of, and why.

Then engage them in a discussion in order to achieve consensus on three things to stop, three to start, and three to continue or expand. To ensure that everyone's voice is heard, it may be best to start with small group discussions with 4–5 people, or even a private discussion board where individuals can post their responses for others to see. (If you are concerned about candor and not worried about civility, you can allow anonymous posts on the bulletin board so people say what's on their minds.)

In the years that we have conducted this activity with groups all over the country, one item crops up consistently: reading.

"**Reading** is fundamental" has been repeated so often that it has become a cliché. Unlike a lot of clichés, this one is true. It's always high on teachers' lists because if kids can't read, they can't do required class work. Even the most poorly educated parents also understand that their kids have to learn to read in order to be successful at practically anything. Consider these research results summarized by Levenson (2012):

- A student who can't read on grade level by third grade is four times less likely to graduate by age 19 than one who does read proficiently by that time. Add poverty to the mix, and a struggling reader is 13 times less likely to graduate on time than his or her proficient and wealthier peer. Yet 89% of students in poverty who do read on level by third grade graduate on time.

- Nationwide, reading is the core challenge for 40% of all students in special education. Fully 80% of students with the designation SLD (specific learning disability) struggle with reading. SLD is the largest disability group, accounting for over 40% of students receiving special education services.

The point is that reading is a sound investment in both student achievement and overall school performance. The earlier and more intensive the intervention, the more effective it is. So solid reading instruction is worth protecting, even extending, in the face of budget reductions.

For elementary schools, the message is pretty clear: reading is central in the primary grades. For middle and high school leaders, the challenge is somewhat greater, but the earliest intervention possible—like during a student's first year in the school or even during the summer before entry—is the best investment. And it needs to be intensive, involving explicit instruction, tutoring, and lots of practice.

From a fiscal point of view, a solid foundation in reading will help eliminate the need for a lot of other remedial, dropout prevention, or other costly interventions later on in the student's school career.

Integrate Technology Thoughtfully. Since schools began to use computer-based instruction the 1970s, we have been warned that "machines can never replace teachers." While that's still true, the judicious use of technology can extend the reach of good teachers, help individualize instruction for diverse student groups, make instruction much more engaging and realistic, and, frankly, save money (Petrilli & Roza, 2011).

Two recent developments, hybrid classes and "flipped" instruction, both of which have been used in higher education for some time, have helped to bring about more effective technology use in K-12 schools as well.

- " 'Hybrid' or 'Blended' are names commonly used to describe courses in which some traditional face-to-face 'seat time' has been replaced by online learning activities. The purpose of a hybrid course is to take advantage of the best features of both face-to-face and online learning. A hybrid course is designed to integrate face-to-face and online activities so that they reinforce, complement, and elaborate one another, instead of treating the online component as an add-on or duplicate of what is taught in the classroom" (University of Wisconsin—Milwaukee, 2013). The bottom line is that more students often can be served in a hybrid course than in more conventional models.

- " 'Flipping the classroom' means that students gain first exposure to new material outside of class, usually via reading or lecture videos, and then use class time to do the harder work of assimilating that knowledge, perhaps through problem-solving, discussion, or debates" (Brame, 2013). Usually, these kinds of experiences are arranged within an online course management system that allows students to have access from anywhere with an internet connection.

Both of these approaches, as well as the ones recommended by Petrilli (2012) that follow, allow for more efficient use of time and opportunities for cost savings.

- Teach foreign languages using Rosetta Stone or some other online software system instead of a conventional classroom. This broadens the number of offerings available and allows students to progress at their own pace.

- Arrange for students to receive on-line tutoring from low-cost college students, retirees, or volunteers rather than pricier full-time employees.

- Divide [larger] classes in half with one group receiving online instruction and the other working with a first-rate teacher.
- Stretch three elementary teachers across four classrooms by rotating students through an online learning lab staffed by an aide.

Clearly some of these approaches require up-front investments that may not be available in the current climate, although by consolidating dispersed resources (such as computer equipment), it may be possible to create facilities that support greater technology use.

Social Resources

Social resources are the community assets that help schools do a better job. Typically, these resources fall into two categories: partnerships and community connections.

A Range [Bidding] War

A Wyoming principal was asked to speak to an agribusiness group about how his school helped prepare graduates for work in their field. He described their biology programs, their agriculture curriculum, and some of the extra-curricular programs focused on agriculture. Then he added that he thought too much of the program was classroom based because the school lacked facilities for more hands-on, field-based work.

One builder immediately volunteered to provide a greenhouse to support the school's programs. Not to be outdone, two water specialists offered an irrigation system for the greenhouse and an adjoining garden plot. Finally, a local grower chipped in seeds, growing media, and potting supplies, and promised to buy healthy school-grown plants at competitive prices for resale in her business.

Somewhat dazed, the principal left the lunch meeting with thousands of dollars worth of contributions to the program. It wasn't bad for 60 minutes of public relations work!

Partnerships are essentially organized ways of using community assets to increase a school's resources and achieve its goals. They are such a vital strategy in helping schools adjust to the New Normal that we devote an entire chapter in this book to partnerships and sponsorships.

For the purposes of this chapter, it is important to begin thinking about potential partners and how they might support the school's mission. Every community has different partnership assets, and wise school leaders spend time cultivating relationships with those potential partners in a systematic and planned manner. Groups that might partner with the school don't necessarily hang around schools waiting to be asked for help, so leaders need to go where the potential partners are: civic clubs, chambers of commerce, or other business or nonprofit gatherings.

Never turn down an invitation to talk about the school to a civic group, service club, or other potential partners. In fact, one of your first partnerships might be with a local media firm that can help develop a short, engaging, information-rich video presentation that you or the leadership team could use for civic presentations instead of a conventional "speech" (which most adults will do almost anything to avoid). You might even start a bidding war that benefits the school in tremendous ways—like the example from Wyoming in the "Range [Bidding] War" box.

The "STOP, START, CONTINUE" exercise at the end of this chapter has a partnership component that encourages you and your leadership team to begin to plan, systematically, to seek out partners and partnerships and sponsorships, provides more explicit strategies for cultivating the social resources of the community in order to benefit students.

A Final Word

Some of the refining strategies in this chapter are intriguing and may be feasible in your current situation. Others are certainly more challenging—and may even be infuriating—because they reduce so much of what educators do because of their passion to cold, hard financial decisions and cost-benefit calculations.

Certainly, some areas are simply too complicated to address strictly at the building, or even the district, level. Special education, for example, is such a complex mix of pedagogical science, law, regulation, and emotion that it is almost impossible to make major adjustments at the school level. Teacher compensation plans are similar and are unlikely to be changed very much by individual principals without huge changes in district or state law and policy.

But even within the confines of law, policy, regulation, and custom, individual school leaders still have some latitude in making changes that can, indeed, save precious resources and even improve things for kids. As Rahm Emanuel said, and we quoted earlier, "never let a good crisis go to waste."

Think About It: "What If" Scenarios

Take some time to consider "what if" scenarios that might occur in your school. Start with the most probable ones based on your current knowledge: "What if Mr. B (the math teacher) retires this year and we don't have money to fill the position?" "What if I have to find a $25,000 savings. Where will we find it?" Use a simple tool like this one to record your thoughts and brainstorms.

What if . . .	We could . . .
Mr. B retires from the math department.	
We are told to find a one-time $25,000 savings in next year's budget.	

Then engage your leadership team in the discussion. Focus on maintaining services, if at all possible, with less money. Consider the strategies in this chapter as ways to achieve school goals without the resources you currently have. Also, think about partners and community connections that might help meet these new challenges.

Now Try This
A Stop/Start/Continue Discussion with the Leadership Team

Engage your leadership team in a discussion about what your school needs to stop doing, start doing, and continue doing—and how you might engage in productive partnerships to make it happen.

Set the Context

Ask your school leaders to think about what you are currently doing in your school by asking them to reflect on these questions:

- What is not working in our school? (Something we should STOP).
- What should we put in place to improve things? (Something we should START).
- What is working well and should be continued? (Something we should CONTINUE).

Seek Agreement

Now have a discussion to identify three things the group believes you could STOP, three you should START, and three you should CONTINUE.

Identify Potential Partners

Work together to identify potential partners—businesses, nonprofits, or other agencies, that might help achieve these changes.

- *Who can help you STOP something?* Can a local community recreation center take on an intramural program that the school can no longer afford? Can a community college offer dual credit courses to replace advanced courses the school can no longer offer?
- *Who can help you START something?* Can you create a compelling vision for a new initiative that a partner might be willing to support or fund? Make sure to identify partners who might have a vested interest in the project.
- *Who can help you CONTINUE something?* Can a booster group take on a specific, valuable program and help raise the resources for it (much the way music programs have operated for many years)? Who in the community has a natural interest in sustaining the program?

7 | Reprioritize School Goals and Functions

Virtually every school district in the country is dealing with the need to reduce their budget. The process for making those decisions varies from district to district but almost always includes a combination of short- and long-term approaches. Once the district has reduced individual budget line items and left vacant positions unfilled there is often a need to look more closely at individual programs and practices and think about reprioritizing them.

In others, the approach is to look more wholly at the mission and vision of the district and align expenditures with that mission and vision. Invariably, interest groups seek to minimize reductions to their favored programs by lobbying the superintendent and Board of Education, and parent and community groups advocate for favorite programs.

Confounding the issue is the need to continue reducing the budget in an environment of stable or declining resources. Most school districts have repeatedly made reductions only to find they need to plan for further budget cuts. In most cases, reductions have occurred for several years and are now a routine part of the annual budgeting process.

As a result of the current financial crisis the easiest, least disruptive, reductions have already taken place. Further reductions will require a more complex process of assessing the contribution of every function to the core mission of schools and balancing competing interests.

Leading the Conversation

There is no single process that makes decisions about reducing budgets acceptable. Because school districts are comprised of varied interest groups, all with a vested interest in the district's programs and practices, the process is often highly politicized. Bolman and Deal (2008) suggest that organizations are most political when confronted by scarce resources like money. The tension around budget priorities, in a very politicized environment, leads to conflict among groups. The result is intense bargaining, negotiating and jockeying for position to minimize the impact on favored programs.

That's what makes a conversation about reprioritizing useful. It allows a school or district to work with stakeholders like teachers and families to fundamentally examine some of its core operations and consider ways to sustain those functions while also dealing with declining resources. When districts consider reprioritizing they generally consider four factors:

- Existing and proposed programs with attention paid to any that are mandated by state or federal law.
- The district's financial strengths and projected needs.
- Any collective bargaining agreements and other contractual obligations.
- Projected revenues.

Districts use a variety of approaches and weigh the four factors differently.

Long Term or Short Term

Faced by the perennial need to reduce budgets many schools and districts face the need to adopt a long-term budgeting process that focuses on a mutually agreed upon mission and vision for the district. Unfortunately because of the contentious nature of any discussion about budgets many schools and districts choose to look for short-term solutions that may solve the immediate financial problem but do little to advance the district's mission and vision.

Because the current financial climate may reflect the long-term reality for most public schools, groups like the National School Boards Association (www.nsba.org) and the Association of School Business Officials (www.asbointl.org) recommend that schools and districts adopt a long-range budget planning process, one that includes identifying the school/district's core mission and vision, and a process to carefully assess the contributions of every function to that mission. In other words, they encourage schools and districts to review and reprioritize their operations.

Checklist for Budget Planning

_____ Do we have a plan for focusing on long-term budget planning rather than short-term decisions?

_____ Do we have an agreed upon mission and vision for our school or district?

_____ How will we gather data about our programs and services so that we can assess their effectiveness?

_____ What process will we use to reach our budget planning decisions?

Getting Started

While no process to reduce budgets is described as ideal, there are several characteristics of those that are less contentious. Part IV of this book includes several tools that leaders can use to lead collaborative and inclusive efforts.

Use an Inclusive Process

Involving all stakeholders builds greater support and commitment to the outcomes of any budgeting process. While the final decision always rests with the superintendent and Board of Education, it is important to identify a way to engage constituents in the process. Many districts find it helpful to have a budget advisory committee, or to convene a group of stakeholders to suggest recommendations to the Board of Education.

Once such a group is convened it is important to be clear about how the collaboration will take place. It can be helpful to have an agreed upon set of norms about group operations and decision making. Garmston and Wellman (1999) suggest seven norms of collaboration that can make discussion, particularly about contentious issues, more productive. Information about the norms, including a self-assessment for use by any group, is available at http://www.thinkingcollaborative.com/norms-collaboration-toolkit/.

Facilitators	Barriers
• Adequate time to meet, discuss, plan, and assess current programs • Clear understanding of the areas/topics to be addressed • Accountability and responsibility of participants • Available data about current programs and conditions • Clarity about decision-making process	• Short timeline or no clarity about time to complete work • Task unclear or ill defined • Limits on decision making unclear or undefined • Reliance on opinions rather than data

Maintain an Open, Transparent Process

Nothing detracts more from a successful budgeting process than the appearance that decisions are made without sufficient public involvement and knowledge. Provide a mechanism to both gather and share information with constituent groups. Conduct all meetings in public and share information about those meetings. As you make decisions about reductions be sure that you are able to explain the rationale for why each reduction is recommended.

Think About It

1. If you were creating a group to help you make decisions about reprioritizing, what groups should be represented? Are there individuals who are open to all points-of-view and would be good at listening and generating alternatives?

2. Are there "movers and shakers," recognized leaders in your community or people others turn to for guidance on important issues who should be involved? If so, who are they? What expertise or skills might they add to a collaborative group?

Align Budget with Mission and Vision of the District

While difficult to do in a highly politicized environment, the most successful budgeting processes occur when the district has a clearly articulated mission and vision that was mutually agreed to by constituent groups. When reductions are needed, it is easy to select options that may detract from your mission and vision. For example, choosing to eliminate all vacant positions may, depending on the vacancy, reduce staffing for vital programs that are key to achieving your vision. More challenging is to reduce staff in less vital programs and functions and use those savings to fund positions in programs needed to achieve your vision. Tools for developing a shared vision are included in Part IV of this book.

Recognize the Importance of Communication

Resistance tends to be greater when people feel uninformed and lack information about both the process and the results. When making budgeting decisions, it is important to provide constituents with useful information. For example, you might want to provide information about how schools are funded in your state, why there is a need for reductions (slow economy, state funding cuts, rising health care costs), how the financial crisis affects your school (amount of reduction), and what reductions you've made in prior years. You will also want to share the budget planning timeline including how citizens and employees can be involved and how to suggest reductions.

Checklist of Communication Considerations

_____ Do we have a process for routinely communicating with constituents about budget planning and decisions?

_____ How will we both gather and share information?

_____ How might we use social media to engage constituents in the budget planning process? (see Part IV)

_____ What is our plan for using and responding to this information?

Common Approaches to Reprioritizing

While every district designs its own process for reprioritizing, there are some common approaches. In many districts most of these approaches have already been used.

Low-Hanging Fruit

In orchards some trees have branches that animals and humans can reach with little effort. The fruit on these branches may be easier to harvest and is commonly called "low-hanging fruit." In budgeting, the term is used to identify items in a budget than might be easily "harvested" without significantly disrupting the operation of the school or district. Two common examples include reducing office supplies or increasing the cost of school lunches. The problem with "low-hanging fruit" is that most of these reductions have little impact on the overall budget and many of them may only be "harvested" once, they are not ongoing budget expenditures. In most schools and districts, most of the "low-hanging fruit" has been harvested.

Rethinking Current Programs or Functions

Another strategy is to rethink some of the fundamental operations of the school or district. In many states it is possible to rethink the organization of the school day or school week. In fact over 120 districts in 21 states currently use a four-day week schedule instead of the traditional five-day model (National Conference of State Legislatures, 2010).

Four-Day Week

In Oregon several districts adopted a four-day week by lengthening each of the four remaining days. They maintain the same hours of instruction but spread it over four days. Each day is longer. The district saves on related costs for transportation, clerical, food service, heating, and other functions. In some schools the fifth day is devoted to more focused teacher and administrator planning and professional development that positively impacts student learning.

Recent evidence from Colorado shows a positive impact on student learning when the four-day week is implemented. While parents, teachers, and students generally feel positive about the four-day week, classified staff, the employee group most impacted, often reacts negatively. Other issues include concerns about childcare demands for parents, and students' ability to handle a longer school day.

Some districts have begun to examine other practices that have been long accepted as the norm. For example, principals may serve more than one school, professional development may be shared with other districts, or curriculum development may be done in conjunction with a consortium of districts or with a nearby college or university. In Michigan it is common for regional educational service agencies to organize professional training and extend invitations for local school districts to enroll teachers in the training. This model allows smaller districts to pool their resources to tap into needed training.

Math Across the Curriculum

Traditionally, mathematics was taught during math class and language arts was taught during language arts. But the move to adopt the Common Core State Standards has encouraged many schools to look for ways to teach subjects "across the curriculum" and to build interdisciplinary application into their curriculum.

At Parker Memorial School in Tolland, Connecticut, teachers have developed a set of lessons that integrate math instruction and application into subjects like literature, history, science and geography as well as music, art, and health classes. For example, when students study rhythm they learn that musical notes represent time and how harmony is an application of the concept of ratio. Students also compose a short musical selection and discuss how they applied time and ratio to the piece.

Other districts reduce transportation costs by only providing transportation for elementary and middle school students. The Ann Arbor (MI) Public Schools worked with the local transportation agency to provide high school students with free bus passes that they could use on routes to and from school. Yet others rely on booster groups to fund extracurricular activities.

Time as a Resource

Middle and high school schedules are often thought of as fixed, with uniform class periods meeting the same time each day. But some principals think about the schedule, and the use of time, as a resource. They work with their staff to rethink the school day, often allowing them to add classes, or add times to existing subjects. Here are some of the options being used.

Block—These schedules provide long instructional blocks that teachers can use for greater instructional flexibility. Removing the boundary of a fixed period schedule allows greater creativity, permits interdisciplinary instruction, and promotes application of student learning.

4 x 4 Block—This schedule is most common in high schools. Each class is longer and fewer classes (4) meet each day. Classes often meet only for a single semester rather than an entire year. It gets the benefits of the block schedule described earlier and provides greater flexibility in scheduling teachers, particularly if they are shared among more than one school.

Alternating Day—Classes do not meet every day but alternate every other day. Sometimes there are longer blocks but not always. Alternating day schedules allow students to take more classes or as a way to provide additional support for students.

Trimester—The school year is divided into three equal parts in a trimester schedule. It allows a student who fails to recover faster and provides greater flexibility in scheduling teachers because some classes meet one trimester, some two, and a few meet all three trimesters. Generally each individual class is longer than a traditional class period and there are fewer each day.

Adapted from: Williamson's *Scheduling to Improve Student Learning* (2009).

Retraining and Cross-Training

As resources shrink many districts have begun to consider how they can retrain or cross-train employees. Most commonly used with classified staff retraining is designed to provide flexibility in scheduling and use of employees. Many employee groups, however, like the benefits of cross-training because it is an alternative to being downsized, becoming a part-time employee, or losing your job.

Cross-Training, or retraining, doesn't work for every employee or position due to specific knowledge and skills required for some positions. In some counties in North Carolina, it was common for school bus drivers to also work as a lunch room supervisor or as a teacher aide. The benefit to the employee is full-time work, and the district benefits by reducing turn-over among employees.

But cross-training does not just occur with classified staff. Some districts have begun to help teachers retrain in other content areas. For example, there is an emphasis in some states for teachers of a foreign language to be able to teach multiple languages, or for a special education teacher to work with students of multiple disabilities. Such flexibility benefits both the employee and the employer. In the College of Education at Eastern Michigan University, there is a recognition that one way for a student to make themselves more marketable, and therefore more likely to be employed, is to be able to teach in more than one content area.

Outsourcing

Outsourcing refers to the practice of using an external company to provide services that may currently be provided by district employees. Many school districts have chosen to focus on the core function of teaching and learning and outsource custodial, maintenance, food service, transportation, human resources, and payroll functions. While outsourcing is an attractive option, it almost always includes lay offs of current employees, an option that may be difficult in some communities where school jobs come with stable employment, good fringe benefits, and comfortable salaries. Most districts that outsource negotiate an agreement with the external company to hire current district employees displaced by the outsourcing.

Consolidating or Shared Services

Yet another approach has been for several contiguous districts to work together on some functions in order to reduce expenditures. Like outsourcing, the most common areas of consolidation include transportation, food service, custodial, and maintenance services. In some states, regional education agencies provide services that traditionally have been conducted in individual school districts. The Michigan legislature provides incentives for school districts to consolidate some of these "back office" functions and devote district resources to the core functions of teaching and learning.

However, a number of school districts have begun to share teaching and administrative staff as well. Some teachers are employees of one district but work in other districts to provide specific services or instruction. This is most often the case when teaching a highly specialized curricular area or when providing services for handicapped students. Several smaller districts in the Midwest have shared superintendents. Generally one school district contracts with a neighboring district to provide the administrative services.

Embracing Technology

Another way to reduce expenditures is to use technology as a tool to replace instruction in specific content areas. For example, Utah provides an *Electronic High School* (www.schools.utah.gov/ehs/) that makes classes available to students in every region of the state. It is designed to provide classes that may not be available in the local school district and also offers a way for students to accelerate their graduation from high school or to recover from failed classes. *Oregon Online* (www.o2learning.org/welcome.html) provides over 70 online courses for high school students in many content areas including world languages and advanced mathematics.

In southwestern Oregon a consortium of small, rural schools worked together to secure funding to offer online instruction in several subjects like Spanish, calculus, physics, and chemistry. Individually, no school had sufficient enrollment to allow them to provide the course. But together they had enough students to be able to offer the courses. The goal was to have instruction online and have teachers of those courses rotate among the four schools.

Securing Other Funding

Other strategies can be used to secure additional funding. The first involves diversifying funding streams. Look for other public funding, seek grants from private foundations, and conduct direct fundraising. The second is to coordinate funding from various sources that may be targeted at specific populations of students. For example, blending categorical funding for Title I, Head Start, IDEIA's Grants for Infants and Families with Disabilities, and Social Services Block Grants. Federal legislation, including NCLB, provide provisions allowing more blending of funding streams.

The same consortium of Oregon districts that are working on online courses pooled their resources to hire a part-time grants writer. The sole purpose of the position is to identify and secure funding for creative and innovate programs across the four districts.

Build Consensus

The challenge when you engage and involve stakeholders in work to reprioritize your budget is reaching agreement on recommendations. Even when it is clear that the superintendent and Board of Education will make final decisions, groups grapple with the process of discussing the issues and reaching agreement on recommendations.

Decisions about budget priorities are not simple. They involve assimilating a lot of information about many different kinds of programs, then examining a variety of options and working to synthesize the information and make an informed decision.

There's evidence that groups of stakeholders who have an interest in a topic can often make better, more informed decisions, than a single individual. Further, many decisions require "buy in" from stakeholders, the people who may be affected by the decision. So, there's good reason to involve people in a decision to reprioritize your budget.

The dilemma you create when involving others is the need to have a clear process for working together, an understanding of the role of the group, and a way to make decisions.

Consensus Building and Decision-Making Tools

The evidence is clear that working with stakeholders can build greater support and commitment for any initiative. Any discussion about declining resources invariably provokes defensiveness and people may choose to protect programs and practices they favor.

We've learned that a collaborative approach is far more productive. While collaboration won't ensure agreement, it does create the conditions where it is possible to talk about difficult and contentious issues and seek a mutually agreed upon resolution. Better decisions generally emerge from a collaborative process because of the different perspectives that are shared.

A collaborative process also contributes to better relationships among members. The process includes listening to varied points-of-view and working together to propose a solution. Finally, when groups are involved in proposing solutions, they are more likely to support implementation. A collaborative process can minimize those who work to undermine or sabotage the solution.

Whom to Involve—When convening any group it is important to consider who should be involved. It is important to include stakeholders who will be impacted by a decision as well as those responsible for implementing any decision. It's unlikely that every person who will be impacted by a decision can be involved so it is important to think about how to determine involvement.

How to Determine Involvement	
Involve	Does the person/group have a stake in the outcome and have some level of expertise?
Don't Involve	Is this person/group indifferent to the outcome and have no expertise?
Limited Involvement	Does the person/group have concerns about the outcome but lack expertise or is indifferent to the outcome?

Source: Williamson and Blackburn (2010) and Adapted from Hoy and Tarter (2008).

Use Norms of Collaboration—It is helpful to have an agreed upon set of norms for how a group will operate and make decisions. Too often there is an assumption that members of a group will respect one another and the differing points-of-view that may be present. But the presence of a set of norms can really promote thoughtful, and collegial, discussion.

We're fans of the *Seven Norms of Collaboration* developed by Garmston and Wellman (1999). Information about the norms including a tool to conduct a self-assessment is available at www.thinkingcollaborative.com/norms-collaboration-toolkit/.

Be Clear about the Task—Perhaps the most important part of collaborative planning is to be clear about the task. Most groups are far more productive when there is a clear statement of the purpose of the group and any timelines for concluding the work. Educators are known for their ability to "talk an issue to death" and being clear about the task (what is to be done) and the timeline for completing the task helps keep a group focused.

Select a Decision-Making Process—It's also important to be clear about how decisions will be made. Most groups want clarity about who will decide and the role of the group. Is the group providing input? Helping to narrow options? Making a recommendation?

It is always better to be clear about decision making at the beginning of collaborative work rather than at the end. Consensus is always a good model but sometimes that doesn't work well for a group. Regardless of the model, being clear at the onset of the work is helpful.

Voting can be a good option when opinions are strongly divided between options. But voting almost always creates winners and losers. There are other decision-making tools that can help a group make decisions.

One alternative is multi-voting. It works well when you want to narrow the options. Each participant receives a certain number of votes in each ballot and you conduct multiple rounds of voting. Participants can give one vote to several options or all of their votes to a single item. Multi-voting often reduces the number of people who have not cast a single vote for the final option.

One of our favorite decision-making methods is the "Fist to Five" (Fletcher, 2002). It's an easy way to assess the level of support for any alternative and can help a group move toward consensus. When using "Fist to Five," ask every participant to raise their hand and indicate the level of support from a closed fist (no support) to all five fingers (I really like this idea).

Fist to Five	
Fist	No support—"I need to talk more."
1 finger	No support but I won't block—"I still need time to discuss the issues and will suggest changes."
2 fingers	Minimal support—"I am moderately comfortable with the idea but would like to discuss minor changes."
3 fingers	Neutral—'I'm not in total agreement but feel comfortable to let the idea pass."
4 fingers	Solid Support—"I think it's a good idea and will work for it."
5 fingers	Strong Support—"It's a great idea, and I will be one of those working to implement it."

Source: Williamson and Blackburn's *Rigorous Schools and Classrooms: Leading the Way* (2010).

Reaching Consensus—*The American Heritage Dictionary* (2013) defines consensus as "an opinion or position reached by a group as a whole." In consensus decision making, it is generally believed that everyone participating in the decision should agree with the decision and/or commit to not interfere with it's adoption. In other words, everyone can "live with it."

When reprioritizing a budget there can be strongly held opinions because of the way budget decisions can impact individuals, their children's education, or their employment. Consensus, while ideal, can be difficult to achieve. That's why we described a couple of other options earlier in the chapter. But if you are committed to a consensus model, here are some things to keep in mind.

- Understand that consensus decision making involves including all relevant stakeholders, and every stakeholder included in the group is obligated to contribute their opinions and suggestions. Everyone must be willing to collaborate by listening, asking questions, and proposing solutions that will satisfy everyone in the group.

- No individual's opinions or suggestions are more important than those of anyone else. The goal is a common solution, even though there will be differences among individuals in the group. The intent is to reach agreement on a decision everyone can accept, not one that meets every member's needs.

- Before you begin, decide how the group will make decisions. Many groups require every member to be satisfied with the decision. Other groups use other options like a super-majority. Regardless of what you decide, it must be clear when you begin the work.

- Make sure members understand what it means to agree. Consenting to the proposed solution doesn't mean it's your preferred choice. Members should share their concerns prior to moving toward agreement.

- Be clear about what is to be decided before you begin. Members deserve to know the limits on the topic and any parameters that may shape solutions. For example, in many reprioritizing discussions, solutions cannot be more costly than the things they replace.

- Once the work begins, place a high value on open and honest, but thoughtful and respectful discussion. Before moving toward a decision, assess the level of support. That's where a tool like the "Fist to Five," described earlier, can be useful. If agreement is not present, or close, continue the work.

- When you seek agreement, always use the decision-making process selected earlier. Never impose a new process when finalizing the work.

Consensus Decision-Making Options

- Absolute Consensus—Agreement by every member.

- All But One—A single dissenter can't block the decision but can ask for more discussion and must provide their reasons for not agreeing. The group then considers these reasons.

- All But Two—Most groups recognize that when two members don't agree there must be further discussion. Dissenters must explain why they can't agree and suggest an alternative solution.

- All But Three—When three or more cannot agree that generally means the group must continue to discuss the issues and modify the proposed solution.

- Super-Majority—Many groups decide that when 60% or more of the group agrees they have achieved a solution.

- Simple Majority—This option is rarely used in a consensus model and is similar to voting.

Cope with Dissent

Virtually any attempt to reorganize and restructure a school district prompts dissent. But the amount of dissent and its intensity is greater when you're reprioritizing things while dealing with declining resources.

Dissent is often a valuable way for stakeholders to raise questions, request information, insist on participation, and even slow or alter outcomes. American political tradition respects the right of stakeholders to speak and to be heard.

Dissent and resistance are often rooted in feelings and beliefs, not information on data. That makes them difficult to address. It's often helpful to allow people to clarify their feelings and allow them time to work through their concerns. Doing so recognizes that schools are human enterprises staffed with individuals who hold passionate perspectives on a school's programs and practices.

While some people resist almost everything, most don't. Most dissenters hold genuine concerns about a proposal particularly if they believe that it will negatively impact students or their own livelihood.

There are often diverse feelings and concerns when you begin to reprioritize school programs. Personal concerns often dominate early discussion;

as the process evolves, concerns about managing and implementing the change come to the fore. Leaders must recognize these steps, outlined by Hord, Rutherford, Huling-Austin, and Hall (1987).

Value of Dissent

Being criticized, questioned, and challenged never feels good, but dissent is a necessary and valuable part of the process. Former Superintendent Richard Benjamin often remarked that "our critics are our friends." What he meant was that critics often raise legitimate questions and force planners to be more thoughtful in their work.

Questions and concerns raised by dissenters are often a barometer of community feeling and can serve as an "early warning system" for school leaders.

Understanding Resistance

Too often dissent is treated as irrational and counterproductive. Ignoring, or pretending there is no dissent, simply provides another issue: not being listened to. An alternative is to treat dissent as rational. Legitimize dissent and turn it to your advantage.

Listen for "key" ideas during meetings. Ask clarifying questions. Use neutral non-inflammatory language. Often dissent is based on feelings and beliefs, an individual's perception of what is happening. While these perceptions may not be accurate, they must still be addressed. Don't take criticism personally and make a good faith effort to respond to questions and deal with the issue.

A good strategy is to ask people to write their comments or questions. Putting their thoughts on paper provides an opportunity to lessen some of the emotion. It also provides a process to gather community input and allows you to target information at specific constituent groups.

Turning Dissent into Support

Incorporating several strategies into the planning can minimize the impact of dissenters.

Include Dissenters—It is far more difficult to criticize a plan when you've been part of the process. People support things they've been part of creating. Including dissenters will not stifle dissent but it provides a legitimate, authentic forum for discussion. Further, including critics signals that there isn't a predetermined solution and the process is not designed to "rubber-stamp" a plan.

Allow Adequate Time—Don't rush into making decisions. Allow sufficient time so that the issues can be adequately discussed. Provide time to both gather and share information and to allow for consideration of alternatives.

Be Open about Advantages and Disadvantages—Recognize that almost every plan has costs as well as benefits. Don't try and portray a new priority as perfect or idea. Have an open, honest discussion of the advantages and disadvantages. Acknowledge and discuss each in the context of student needs and limited resources.

Clarify the Issues—When reprioritizing, "real" issues will emerge. They often concern fundamental issues about the viability of an idea, or implementation of an alternative. But it is also common for issues to emerge that mask the true motives. When Ron helped a Chicago area middle school redesign it's schedule, exploratory teachers (art, music, technology) shared their concern that their content was being marginalized in the new schedule. After talking with the teachers it was clear the "real" issue was whether they would continue to have a job. Resolving that issue helped each of them to think creatively about how to make the new schedule work.

Think About It

1. Consider your school, district, and community. What's the pattern of resistance to changes in school programs? What advice would you offer yourself about learning from those experiences when reprioritizing your budget?

2. What previous strategies have been successful at minimizing dissent and resistance? Which ones would you want to use when reprioritizing your budget?

Engaging Staff and Community

Throughout this chapter we've discussed the value of involving stakeholders, staff, and community, when reprioritizing your budget. A collaborative process is important but it's also important to develop a plan to engage the entire staff and the larger community.

It's a form of planned community engagement and recognizes that staff, families, and community all have a vested interest in decisions about reprioritizing. There needs to be opportunities to both share information and to gather information from these groups. One of the things every school leader knows is that the conversation about their school or district is already happening. What leaders want to do is be part of the conversation so that they can help their community deal with the challenges of reprioritizing a budget.

Multiple Audiences

Every school community is composed of a variety of stakeholder groups. There are groups of "internal" employees and "external" groups such as parents and segments of the larger community. Each of these audiences has a different need for information and involvement.

Even then, groups, like employees or parents, can be subdivided into other smaller subgroups. That means that the message and the delivery may need to be tailored to each group. Some groups may prefer regular newsletters or online updates. Other groups may prefer a combination of paper materials and face-to-face meetings. What's most important is to recognize the unique needs of each group and to tailor your plans to fit each group.

Parents and Families—We know that parents are important allies. They can be advocates for your school with extended family, friends, and community. In many states, parents have choices about where they send their children to school, and you want to ensure that they have the information they need to continue to send their children to your school.

- **Communicate Often**—You just can't communicate enough with families. But be sure you provide them with the information they need and make sure you provide details about how they can be involved and how they can share their opinions.

- **Use Social Media and Other Online Media**—Many families rely on social media and other online tools as a primary source of information (Brenner & Smith, 2013). In Part IV, we discuss online tools that many schools use to engage families. But be cautious about over-relying on technology. Many families still have limited online access. Use varied ways to communicate with families.

- **Provide Meaningful Involvement**—Parents want to be involved in decisions impacting their child's schooling. Provide meaningful roles for parents beyond traditional PTO and fundraising activities.

Community—The National School Public Relations Association encourages school leaders to create a "Key Communicator Network" to help you share and gather information about your school or district. Communication is a two-way street, and the network is designed to help you share information and gather feedback and suggestions.

If you're the principal of a large school or district, you might use your leadership team as part of the network. Or you might involve an established network of parents or business leaders.

Build a Network

1. Bring together a small group of trusted people who know the community. Brainstorm with them about who are the people whom others listen to. While the bank president may be an opinion leader, so might the barber, cab driver, bartender, or supermarket checkout clerk.

2. Create a list from the names you gather to invite to join your network. Make sure that all segments of the community are represented.

3. Send a letter or e-mail to the potential members explaining that you want to create a group to help you both gather and share information with the community. Invite the potential members to an initial meeting.

4. Make follow-up contact, especially with those who will be most important to have part of the network.

5. Meet with the group and let them know you see them as respected community members who care about the education students are being provided and that you believe schools operate best when the community understands what is taking place and becomes involved in providing the best possible learning opportunities for students. Then, describe the objectives of a Key Communicator Network:

- To provide network members with honest, objective, consistent information about the school or district,

- To have the network members share this information to others in the community when they are asked questions or in other opportunities, and

- To keep their ears open for any questions or concerns community members might have about the work to reprioritize the budget. Those concerns should be shared so that the information can be used to inform the reprioritizing process.

- Ask the invitees for a commitment to serve on the network and find out the best way to communicate with them.

6. Establish a Key Communicator Network newsletter specifically for members and provide them with regular updates on the process.

Adapted from: Williamson and Blackburn's *The Principalship from A to Z* (2009).

For additional information about the *Key Communicator Network*, contact the National School Public Relations Association (www.nspra.org).

Responding to Rumors

One of the hallmarks of reprioritizing is that there will be lots of rumors about what is planned. Even before the work begins, people begin to share concerns that in turn take on a life of their own. Accurate or not, rumors require a response.

The prevalence of social media has made it easier to spawn rumors, which can be spread quickly via texts or social media sites like Twitter and

Facebook. For many school leaders, the issue is how to respond and put rumors to rest.

The National School Public Relations Association (2010) surveyed principals about rumor control and identified six strategies that principals reported as helpful.

- Recognize the need to get timely and accurate information to key audiences quickly. Avoid an emotional response and provide just the facts.
- Assure people that you are aware of the rumor, and that you will deal with it.
- Encourage people to share rumors and to provide you with specific details so that you can determine an appropriate response.
- Communicate quickly when appropriate so that your message is heard rather than a rumor conveyed by others in the community.
- Create a "Fact Check" site on your school or district's website where people can go to get information, or share a rumor and get a response. A series of questions and responses might be posted.
- You must repeatedly address rumors and recognize that everyone doesn't get their information from the same source. Redundancy is important.

Today it is easier than ever for anyone to comment on your school or district. Social media and other forms of media on the internet make it accessible to most people. For many leaders there is a need to respond but that may not be your best choice. Lisa Barone (2009) of Outspoken Media provides suggestions for how you might react.

1. **Listen without reacting**—Look beyond the description of the problem to find the "root" problem and then work to fix it if possible.
2. **Be absolutely honest**—If you're going to respond, be sure to apologize for any mistake. Don't make excuses and don't try to make yourself look like the victim. Be honest about what is happening.
3. **Always remain calm**—Show that you can take criticism well and that you are open to different points-of-view.

4. **Speak like a real person**—People don't respond well when they feel they are being patronized or you think you are smarter than they are. Talk like a real person and use common everyday words. Avoid educational jargon.

5. **Promise to be better**—Always promise to do a better job of listening and provide a sign that you've heard the person and that you care. (Barone, 2009)

Think About It

1. Who would you talk with about building a network?

2. How would you ensure all segments of your community are involved?

3. How will you share your vision, listen, and gather feedback?

4. How might you keep members engaged in the work?

Final Thoughts

The current economic environment means that schools and districts must continue to carefully examine their budgets and identify ways to make reductions while maintaining a quality educational experience for students. The challenge is to sustain the core function of schools—high quality teaching and learning, while prudently managing their budget. The evidence is that schools and districts are most successful when they have a clear mission and vision and always make budgeting decisions that support that mission and vision.

Now Try This

Assess a recent planning activity. What changes in the planning process might you suggest?

Planning Question	Yes	No	Suggestions
Were the critical stakeholders involved?			
Did we have an agreed upon mission/ vision for our school?			

Did we use data and information about current conditions?			
Was there an agreed upon process for making decisions?			
How did we share information about our work with others?			

Adapted from: Williamson and Blackburn's *Rigor in Your School: A Toolkit for Leaders* (2011).

Resources

Leaders "Hip-Pocket" Guide to Collaborative Planning

www.doe.k12.de.us/rttt/lea_pages/files/HipPocket_CPTR.pdf

This guide from the Delaware Department of Education provides a quick synopsis of the research on collaboration and the importance of collaborative planning groups.

Collaborative Planning Toolkit

www.ncwiseowl.org/impact/toolkit.doc

This toolkit was developed by the North Carolina Department of Public Instruction and provides templates, rubrics, and other guides for collaborative work.

Consensus Decision-Making Tools

www.mindtools.com/pages/article/codm.htm

This site from Mind Tools provides a protocol for a consensus decision-making model.

8 Regenerate with Partnerships and Sponsorships

Partnerships and sponsorships are related but somewhat different ways for schools to generate funds for special programs. Within the category of partnerships, there are at least two distinct types: business partnerships and community partnerships.

Business Partnerships

Business partnerships are typically established between a school or district and a local business partner or national partner with a local presence. These partnerships may also be organized around a collaborative group of businesses and nonprofit agencies that seek to support the schools in their community.

The Council for Corporate and School Partnerships (n.d.), founded by Coca Cola, defines partnerships as "a mutually supportive relationship between a business and a school or school district in which the partners commit themselves to specific goals and activities intended to benefit students and schools. In most cases, partnering is a win-win situation for all involved parties. In addition to improving the education experience, the business partners frequently will realize benefits as well, such as enhanced good will and a stronger presence in the community."

The BEPAC Partnership

"You Don't Just Want a Financial Contribution; What's the Catch?"

"Financial resources are great for short-term projects and activities, but our vision is broader. We're also looking for human resources. Are you willing to allow students and teachers into your business to experience a working environment? Meet with new teacher candidates to validate the quality of life Cecil County can offer its employees? Collaborate with other businesses to define the job skills and future trends the marketplace will demand of today's students as tomorrow's job pool? A small commitment of time can make a big difference with young people who are faced with critical decisions regarding career choices."

From Frequently Asked Questions about BEPAC. www.bepac.org/index.html

DuPage (IL) High School's Business-Education Partnership Council is organized by the school district and staffed by the district's information and public affairs officer. The district and local business members meet once a month to explore ways in which the business community can support the school and review the progress of on-going partnerships. The agenda for this council focuses on student achievement, parent involvement, and community outreach.

In Cecil County (MD), the Business and Education Partnership Advisory Council (BEPAC) is organized by local businesses and serves a broad mission: "BEPAC is an organization that serves as a sounding board to the Superintendent of Schools for Cecil County to identify strengths, needs and trends in the area of job readiness and student success upon graduation from high school. Its mission is to promote quality education in the Cecil County Public Schools to prepare students to meet job market needs, select satisfying careers, and be good citizens in our community. The collective talents of the organization (comprised of industrial, technology, financial, retail and manufacturing representatives in our region) provide an invaluable resource to the support of Cecil County students' preparation for the world of work in the twenty-first century" (BEPAC, 2014).

Community Partnerships

Community partnerships bring together the resources of businesses, individual philanthropists, volunteers, nonprofit agencies, law enforcement agencies, churches, schools, social service agencies, service clubs, higher education institutions—just about anyone with an interest in promoting success for children and young people. One of the most established of these partnerships is the Cincinnati Youth Collaborative (CYC, 2013). Founded in 1987, the CYC's mission was: "To try to reduce the rising failure and dropout rates in the Cincinnati Public Schools and to help every youth in Cincinnati realize his or her potential."

Their vision for their community was simple, straightforward, and ambitious:

> that all Cincinnati youth will graduate from high school with the comprehension, desire, and opportunity to realize their full potential—whether that be to assume a productive and satisfying job or go on to higher education. Specifically, the Collaborative was formed to:
>
> - Increase high school graduation rates
> - Improve the overall academic performance of students
> - Increase the number of students attending college, and
> - Increase the number of youth entering the job market. (CYC, 2013)

Now, more than 100 community partners and 1700 volunteers serve hundreds of students in their mentoring and college access programs with impressive results in a challenging urban environment: 95% of CYC seniors graduated from high school, 8 out of 10 of these grads attended college, and more than 85% of CYC students were promoted to the next grade on schedule (CYC, 2013).

Schools Take Initiative

Cincinnati's Youth Collaborative was founded by 30 community members who were concerned about the number of dropouts from the city's public schools. But other schools didn't wait around for something good like the CYC to just happen in their towns. In communities in Texas, California, Illinois, and Florida, schools became catalysts for creating partnerships. In these cases, the schools solicited the help of an individual or small group of community leaders to help them recruit and lead the community partnership. These individuals recruited like-minded community members from their own organizations or from their personal and professional networks, organized and sponsored a first meeting, and helped the school prepare their "pitch" for help. It most cases, it took only one or two committed, energetic community members with a good list of contacts to get things started. The techniques they used are described in detail later in this chapter.

School Foundations

Foundations are legal entities that exist to provide support for any number of deserving causes, many of which focus on education. How to work with foundations will be covered in Chapter 9, but it is important to know that some school districts actually create their own foundations to support educational programs in their district. Creating a foundation requires specialized legal advice and planning, but many communities find that a local attorney will donate that service in the interest of school improvement.

The Fountain Valley School Foundation was created in 1982 to support educational programming in this California district. Their mission is to provide the "extras" that make an educational program vibrant and meaningful for kids. As California districts continue to struggle with reduced state funding, their message to the community is very clear and direct:

> Fountain Valley Elementary School District performed well academically, once again. How do we keep it going with all of the repeated budget cuts? Unfortunately, we are forced to find the funding other places. Teachers are applying for grants, parents support their teachers, and the Fountain Valley Educational Foundation steps in and helps support programs like Science, Music, Art and Technology, among others. But even for non-profits like us, the times are getting harder to fundraise for these programs. But we cannot give

up, for this is our future we are talking about! Our students, our community, our concern.

So we at FVEF keep working to raise the money required to provide our students with these programs. They need hands-on science to succeed in a medical or research education. When we allow them to learn an instrument, sing in a choir or be a part of a marching band, we give them stepping stones to future success. We give them access to technology, we help prepare them for tomorrow. (Fountain Valley Education Foundation, 2013)

Show Your Support for Education

Most school districts in Florida have educational foundations that are organized to serve the same purpose—to help schools sustain high quality programs in the face of declining public resources. A collaborative effort by these foundations and the Florida Department of Motor Vehicles resulted in the creation of a Florida specialty license plate that generates revenue for district foundations. A portion of the revenue generated by these license tags—about $20—goes to the education foundation in the county where the plate is issued. The program raises more than $1 million annually for these foundations.

The kind of collaboration illustrated by this Florida initiative is rare, but it shows how communities can work together to leverage revenue generating efforts on a grand scale.

Sponsorships

Beyond the advertising and product placement discussed in Chapter 9, many businesses or other organizations will sponsor specific programs, events, or activities that are consistent with either their business interests or their philanthropic goals. Typically, these kinds of sponsorships provide for "naming rights" by the sponsor, so it becomes part of their brand identity.

There are almost as many kinds of sponsorships as there are organizations that sponsor them. They may consist of awards, scholarships, academic programs, capital improvements, after school and enrichment programs, and a huge host of others. The most important consideration about whatever a sponsor chooses to provide is that the project supports the educational program of the school and doesn't distract from or undermine it.

Many sponsorships are not new to schools at all: the Bausch and Lomb Science Award has been in existence since 1933; the American Legion's Boys and Girls State was launched in 1935 and 1937 respectively. Increasingly, though, sponsorships are organized to target specific needs and goals that are perceived either by the sponsoring organization or in response to a school request.

"Enlightened Self Interest"

The Principals' Partnership
A Program of the Union Pacific Foundation

The Union Pacific Foundation Principals' Partnership was a program that provided high-quality professional development and support for 1,000 high school principals in Union Pacific communities from Chicago to the Pacific Coast. The seeds for this program were sown when a UP senior Vice President saw a televised special on the American High School and how tough the principal's job really was. This VP called the program "enlightened self-interest" on the part of the company. They believed that strong leadership builds strong schools that, in turn, contribute to community prosperity and a better-prepared workforce.

In fact, "enlightened self-interest" is among the most powerful motives for corporate or organizational sponsorships. Science, technology, engineering, and math (STEM) programs are sponsored in schools by companies and organizations with a special interest in science and technology. Intel Education supports dozens of activities for K-12 STEM students, as does 3M, Texas Instruments, the American Chemical Society, Apple Computers, and countless others. Science and technology aren't the only beneficiaries of sponsorships, however. Yamaha Music supports music programs for children; Ford Motor Company sponsors design competitions for high school students; *The Nation* magazine runs a writing contest; Crayola created the Arts Inspired Educational Leadership program to promote 21st-century skills. The list of sponsorships is practically endless.

Why Bother?

Why does a company enter into a sponsorship or partnership with schools? Research by the authors (Johnston, 2013) found that there were several categories of motives that explained a large part of corporate giving.

- **Brand Development**. Donors incorporate social investing activities into their brand by creating a visible, admirable philanthropic program with broad, positive appeal and wide dissemination. This builds both brand awareness and consumer allegiance.

- **Improved Public Perception and Reputation**. Social investing can strengthen public perceptions of a company in a particular community or among specific groups. In some cases, it can even repair negative perceptions or help a company prepare for a controversial action. People love stories about their community. So when attractive programs and innovations are reported by local media, it grabs attention and adds to the positive press image of the business sponsor.

- **Long-term Sustainability**. Because business success depends largely on regional success, many companies see philanthropy as an investment in their own success in a region. Stronger communities have more disposable income, which benefits all businesses. Some larger, publically traded companies even note increases in share price as they attract investors from social investment funds and new business in affected communities.

- **Workforce Development**. One of the most significant returns on philanthropy is the development of potential employees. Sometimes, this development occurs because the employer's contributions make it a more "attractive" company, so it draws better applicants. In other cases, a donation may actually strengthen programs—maybe summer camps for kids from low-income families, a reading program at the library, or better lab facilities for the high school—that translate into a better prepared workforce.

- **Employee Satisfaction and Recruitment**. Surveys show that employee performance increases when they believe they work for an employer that "does good" in addition to doing well. In fact, the brightest and most well-prepared graduates list "corporate social responsibility" as one of their top considerations in identifying potential employers.

- **Corporate commitments**. A targeted project may result from a company's dedication to a specific social goal or the passion of a highly placed corporate executive who is committed to a particular field of philanthropy, such as the arts or services for people with disabilities.

Understanding these motives can help schools approach potential partners and sponsors and explain the "return on investment" that company might expect from a partnership with the school community.

The Partnership Dance

[A]n effective partnership is a lot like a dance: Both partners move to the same rhythm and tune, but usually with some improvisation and mutual adjustment as the dance evolves.

As the dancers' relationship matures, the lead may actually shift from partner to partner at specific points in the performance—each one playing to a strength or meeting a specific challenge. Dancers twist and turn to avoid other dancers sharing the floor and adjust to changes in tempo or mood. Eventually, it happens seamlessly and, to outside observers, effortlessly.

Effective partnerships are well-planned (they know in advance if it is to be a waltz or a tango), but they also adjust, quickly, spontaneously, and with a measure of trust, to changing conditions or evolving objectives.

In Atlanta, Superintendent Beverly Hall has attracted more than $156 million in business donations to support her district's key initiatives during the past 10 years. Her advice: "Develop core principles that guide all partnerships, and allow individual schools and business partners to innovate around those core principles" (Johnston, 2009, p. 24).

How to Make It Work

The most comprehensive guide for creating and sustaining strong partnerships is the *How-to Guide for School-Business Partnerships* available free from the Council for Corporate and School Partnerships (n.d.), a group created originally by the Coca Cola Corporation. They describe 18 steps for launching and maintaining productive partnerships, including planning documents and tools that help schools get started and keep potential partners interested in their work. Their key strategies for school leaders include both practical and strategic advice and are summarized here:

1. **Determine if there is a need in the school and if a partnership will help fill those needs.**

Assess Critical Needs. State needs as precisely as possible, then determine what kind of partnership will be most helpful. Does your school need direct contributions? Volunteers? Equipment donations? Professional development in technical areas? Internship placements? What kind of resource will bolster the program to the greatest extent?

Assess Contributors and Contributions. Try to understand how a potential partner's support can make a real difference in meeting a district need. Working together, the school and the partner can determine how to maximize the effectiveness of the partnership and leverage resources.

2. **Identify and research potential partners.**

Tap into available networks. Some of the networks for business and education partnerships are national, but most schools are best served by capitalizing on local networks. Join local service clubs and participate as much as possible; ask parents who work in an organization to put you in touch with their community affairs staff; and most important, develop a 15 second "elevator speech" that can be used to introduce a school need or special project to a potential partner quickly and clearly. In one Colorado high school, the administrators became active in the downtown business association, including sitting on the group's board of directors. They also hosted monthly meetings of the group at the school, which allowed them to show off both their accomplishments and their needs.

Most of all, don't be bashful about discussing the school's needs. After all, it's their community too, and many of them have a deep personal investment in the success of its schools. And don't hesitate to capitalize on internal school resources for finding partners as well. School staff, parent groups, and even students have large networks in the community, so be sure that everyone understand what the school's critical needs really are so they can speak about them intelligently within their own circle of influence.

3. Draft a clear, thoughtful partnership proposal.

Most business-school partnerships are initiated by the schools, so it is important to have a written proposal to share with potential partners. Big companies and foundations will probably require a formal proposal, but for smaller companies or local partners, a straightforward letter of request may suffice. Once a conversation with the potential partner has begun, specific details of the partnership can be negotiated and the terms of the agreement stated with precision.

4. Have a frank discussion about values, goals, and outcomes.

Partnerships are motivated by what's best for students, but partnerships should also be "win-win" arrangements for both the school and the business as well. The pay-off for the business partner may be obvious—such as enhanced reputation in the community—but it may be more subtle as well, such as helping to strengthen the employee pool in a region or creating a corporate image of social responsibility that makes them attractive to young, idealistic employees. The most important idea is to be sure everyone is aware of the pay-off for the partnership, but don't overlook the fact that many companies support schools because they believe it's the right thing to do. A sense of corporate social responsibility is a powerful motive for many organizations to "do good" in addition to "doing well."

5. Establish clear short- and long-term goals for the partnership, agree on outcomes, and assess the impact on a regular basis.

Be sure that goals are important, measurable, and aligned with the mission and purposes of the school. Partnerships that "overlay" existing school programs and activities are often seen as extra work that may not be connected to other goals for which the school is accountable. If a partnership interferes with, or even fails to support, community expectations and state requirements, it is doomed to failure from the outset. It doesn't matter how attractive an add-on partnership program might be, if it doesn't contribute to the school's mission and student welfare, it won't last long.

Assessment of the partnership should be conducted on a regular basis, not only to identify elements in need of adjustment, but also to determine if it is meeting its goals. There are four key areas for assessment and accountability (Johnston, 2009):

Coverage: does the program reach the people it is intended to serve, and does it reach a significant portion of them?

Fidelity: does the program operate as planned and do what it was designed to do?

Impact: does the program achieve the intended outcomes? Are there unanticipated outcomes, both positive and negative, that need to be considered?

Satisfaction: are participants satisfied with the program and pleased with their participation in it?

6. **Integrate the partnership into the school and business cultures, and ensure that partners have a chance to interact with each other.**

Partnerships succeed when they are part of the culture of both organizations. Culture change can be hard to achieve, but one way to bridge the culture divide between businesses and schools is for both partners to learn about and respect the other's norms and operating principles. Four key differences between school and business cultures need to be addressed directly in order for partnerships to succeed.

- **Time**: businesses value quick responses to communication; the business standard is a reply in 24 hours or less. Schools put kids' needs first, so everything else has to wait. That can be frustrating for business partners and harmful to partnerships.

- **Evidence**: businesses value performance metrics—usually quantitative in nature—while schools prize anecdotal evidence that something is working. The solution is to gather both quantitative *and* qualitative data on the partnership. Besides, good anecdotes are helpful to the business partner for their own internal and external public affairs, and good quantitative data can help a school show how a program is working in a very convincing way.

- **Communication**: businesses tend to use a brief, direct, even terse, communication style while school communication is often longer and more oblique. School people may find business communication abrupt, and businesses often see school communication as unclear and ambiguous.

- **Authority and Decision Making**: business decisions are usually made rather quickly by individuals with the authority to do so. Authority in schools is much more "loosely coupled," so school leaders have to work harder at building consensus and agreement—and that takes time. What may appear to a business partner to be a simple decision (such as sending teachers for training) may involve contractual issues, the need to secure qualified substitutes, and a host of other complications that make the school appear to be unnecessarily bureaucratic and unresponsive.

Relationships are the key to successful partnerships and are the basis for solutions to the "cultural divide" problems. Three proven strategies help to bridge these cultures and help sustain healthy partnerships:

- **Designated Contact People**. The single most effective strategy for building and managing an effective partnership is when both partners have a designated contact person who is responsible for staying in touch with his or her partnership counterpart. These individuals ensure that calls and e-mails are returned in a timely manner, that small problems are anticipated and solved, and that routine matters are handled quickly and seamlessly. Champion International Corporation went so far as to house the executive director of their Middle School Partnership in the corporate offices so that he had direct, easy access to key executives.

- **Planned Interactions among Partners**. Planned events allow the partners to build strong relationships, learn more about each other's cultures and goals, and even find new ways to collaborate and expand the partnership. The Union Pacific Principals' Partnership sponsored an annual 4-day summer conference for all 1,000 principals which also included Union Pacific executives and public affairs staff. In addition, UP officials attended regional partnership events provided for the principals so the relationships were reinforced throughout the year. Soon, principals were benefiting from some of the executive training provided by the corporation for their own leaders, and company executives were getting an insider's view of high schools by participating in a "principal for a day" program. The result? A 10-year collaboration that served thousands of principals, tens of thousands of students, and hundreds of school communities across the western United States.

- **Internal and External Public Affairs.** Both partners have an obligation to help the other promote and celebrate the partnership among their constituents. Obviously, the community needs to know about the good things the partners are doing, but sometimes other audiences can be overlooked. Business partners need information and help in promoting the partnership inside their own organizations—to senior executives, shareholders, board members, and employees. For the Pacific Life Nonprofit Internship Experience, program managers produced a "newsletter" version of the annual evaluation report, complete with photos of high school students at their internship sites and testimonials about the program's impact on both the students and the nonprofit organizations. That newsletter was shared internally with Pacific Life executives and staff as well as in the community and among the nonprofit participants, allowing all of them to showcase their roles to their respective clients and constituents.

All of these strategies are designed to keep people informed, ensure that the partnership remains visible in the community, and encourage explicit and enthusiastic support throughout the school and the business—at the highest levels as well as among the staff.

The Power of Relationships

During a severe economic downturn, a major manufacturer had to consider cuts in all of its costs—including the partnership they had with schools in each of their mill locations. On a trip to one mill site, Andy, the CEO, was taken by the mill manager to a local school supported by the company. Expecting to stay for a few minutes, Andy spent three hours visiting the classrooms they helped to improve, observing teachers who did a better job because of the company's support, and talking with kids in this poor community who had superb educational opportunities because of company resources.

At the end of the visit, Andy told the senior executives (and anyone else who would listen), "This entire project in all 65 schools costs less each year than the revenue from one of our mills for one day. We can't possibly do this much good for so many kids for such a small investment in any other way. This program stays."

Partnerships with businesses, nonprofits or other agencies can yield outstanding resources for schools that go well beyond money. It may provide human resources for mentors and tutors, donations of equipment that is outdated for a business environment but perfect for educational purposes, or opportunities for students to engage in "real world" applications of their learning through internships and work-study arrangements.

Sometimes the outcomes of a partnership are unanticipated and still remarkably effective. The superintendent of a large city district in the western United States noticed that many of the district's busses seemed to run only partially full. Given the number of students transported every day, empty seats on busses seemed incongruous with the cost of providing comprehensive bus service. Taking advantage of the district's partnership with a major transportation company, the superintendent asked if the company had "load management" experts who might help them make their bus service more efficient. After studying the problem, the experts suggested a two-pronged approach—new routings that resulted in more students riding each bus, and an in-district marketing and management plan to promote the use of district busses rather than private vehicles. This combined effort not only helped fill the busses, but also eased traffic congestion around district schools during opening and dismissal times. And it all came about because of a relationship between a business partner and a district that was built on trust and a genuine commitment to kids.

Regenerate with Fees, Grants, Contracts, and Entrepreneurial Activity

Budget shortfalls in the past few years have forced school districts to look for new ways to generate revenue for both core programs and extracurricular activities. As a result, schools have either expanded existing revenue-generating programs or have launched major money-making initiatives unlike any that have been used widely in schools before.

Horace Mann's Thoughts on Education

If ever there was a cause, if ever there can be a cause, worthy to be upheld by all of toil or sacrifice that the human heart can endure, it is the cause of Education (Mann, 1872, p. 7).

For many schools and school leaders, this represents a major departure from their traditional roles and responsibilities—a tradition that goes back to Horace Mann's advocacy of the free "common school" in the 1840s. For Mann, and generations of educators trained in the common school philosophy, education was the single greatest good a society could provide, and provide freely, for its children. So, for many educators, the need to raise funds to provide educational opportunities for children flies in the face of nearly 175 years of educational philosophy and social history.

But things have obviously changed in 175 years: demographics, social conditions, economics, technology, and the very nature of schooling itself. And these new conditions require new ways of thinking about more complex problems—the most essential skill required to succeed in the New Normal environment.

This chapter examines three ways schools have used to regenerate resources: fees, grants and contracts, and entrepreneurial activity. All of them have positive and negative aspects, and some are much more familiar to school leaders (fees and grants, for example) than other activities, such as contracts and entrepreneurial programs.

Fees

Despite Mann's admonitions, school fees of various kinds of have been around for a long time, mostly in the form of payments required for specialized extracurricular programs. For decades, students have been required to pay for athletic physicals, musical instruments, field trips, college entrance exams, and a host of other "extras" that helped the school offset costs and still offer full programs. In many cases, fees could be waived for disadvantaged students, or sponsor groups would cover the costs for an entire athletic team, band, or club.

According to the *Wall Street Journal* (Simon, 2011), school fees have expanded exponentially in the past few years:

> Public schools across the country, struggling with cuts in state funding, rising personnel costs and lower tax revenues, are shifting costs to students and their parents by imposing or boosting fees for everything from enrolling in honors English to riding the bus. At high schools in several states, it can cost more than $200 just to walk in the door, thanks to registration fees, technology fees and unspecified "instructional fees."
>
> [Simon adds that although] public schools have long charged for extras such as driver's education and field trips, many are now asking parents to pay for supplies needed to take core classes— from biology-lab safety goggles to algebra workbooks to the printer ink used to run off grammar exercises in language arts. In some schools, each class comes with a price tag, to be paid at registration. Some schools offer installment plans for payment. Others accept credit cards—for a processing fee.

Circles of Caring

Citizens in a Florida Panhandle county formed "Circles of Caring" to provide school fees for kids in need. Housed in churches, civic clubs, firehouses, businesses, and other settings, each "circle" adopts disadvantaged students and ensures that they have the money needed for everything from school fees to social event costs and extracurricular assessments. Volunteers even run a "slightly used" store that provides kids with free prom dresses, tuxedos, and other specialized clothing and equipment that is beyond their families' resources.

Many parents are unhappy about this trend, and some have filed lawsuits challenging the legitimacy of school fees. A new law in California (statute AB1575) bans the collection of fees for classroom instruction and school-sponsored activities, and has left districts scrambling to find money for everything from 25¢ cent pencils to $500 football uniforms. It also prohibits the school from requiring that students bring supplies from home in order to participate in the school's program. All of this stems from a short but powerful line in the California Constitution—the guarantee of "a free public education." The law even bans the use of fees with waivers for disadvantaged youth, and donation campaigns organized by PTAs and booster groups have generally fallen short of replacing lost revenue.

Other states with similar constitutional guarantees are watching with some trepidation to see how the California law finally shakes out at the classroom level. Some already forbid charging fees for basic instructional materials, but still allow fees for extracurricular activities. But even that provision leaves some students disappointed and excluded from everything from school dances to full participation in the extracurricular program.

A junior at one East Bay area high school said she and other students who bought graphing calculators for Algebra II share them with students who are without. Still, she believes students shouldn't have to pay for such things. "It's not really fair," she said, noting many parents are struggling to feed families and can't afford a $100 calculator or other supplies. She applauds the new law and hopes it will be enforced on extracurricular activities—which it covers— because she knows classmates who are shut out of athletics and the annual student dance show because they can't afford the fees (Noguchi, March 2, 2013).

Five Rules for Fees in Schools

1. **Start at the top**. Be sure to check with district officials and legal sources before launching any kind of special fee assessment.

2. **Consider alternatives**. Are there other ways to do this? Other sources of funds? Can you recruit a partner? Can the PTA have a fundraiser? Are grants available? A donor?

3. **Ensure equity**. Will some kids be excluded from activities because of the fees? What can you do to ensure that money alone doesn't determine eligibility?

4. **Do your homework**. Expect pushback from the kids and the community. Make sure you have looked at every alternative and considered all the options.

5. **Consult broadly**. Consult with school leaders, parent groups, advisory councils—anyone who might have a stake in the outcome . . . or an idea for another way of doing things.

In places where they are allowed, fees will almost certainly continue to be collected into the foreseeable future. In Tennessee, fees may be requested but not required, and "payment of 'school fees' may not be a condition to attending the public school or using its equipment (TCA § 49–2-110(c)). In other words, no student may be required to pay fees for workbooks, lab fees, field trips during the school day" (Tennessee State Board, 2009). However, local school boards are given considerable latitude in defining "the school day," so many districts continue to charge for activities outside of normal school hours. Other states are somewhat more permissive, but local pushback and political pressures often trump what is permissible.

Grants and Contracts

The quest for additional resources has led many schools to become much more aggressive about seeking grants and contracts. Grants are non-repayable funds disbursed by one party, often a government department, corporation, foundation or trust, to a recipient, often a nonprofit entity, educational institution, business or an individual. In order to receive a grant, some form of

"Grant Writing," often referred to as either a proposal or an application, is usually required.

Most grants are made to fund a specific project and require some level of compliance and reporting. The grant writing process involves an applicant submitting a proposal to a potential funder, either on the applicant's own initiative or in response to a Request for Proposals from the funder.

Perhaps the most important thing to know about grants is that they require the recipients to do what they promised to do in their proposal. A school cannot decide to use the money awarded for new science lab equipment to fund the music program. Usually, there are no legal consequences for failing to deliver what is promised, but in many cases a clause in the grant will require the school to repay money used in unapproved ways.

Despite the generosity of grantors, grants are not simply large gifts of money that can be used in any way the school sees fit. Some key considerations apply to virtually all grants.

1. **They do not replace general funds**. In most cases, a grant is to do something more than the school is currently doing, not just replace lost funds to keep doing the same things. The loss of funds for the annual ninth grade field trip to the state capitol is probably not going to convince a grantor to provide money to sustain it, *unless* there is some significant new feature to the program—such as shadowing a legislator, or securing meetings with legislators to promote voter awareness among young people.

2. **They restrict how money can be used**. Many grantors will not support capital expenditures, personnel costs (outside of the specific project they are funding), and a host of other items. Be sure to ask for the things the grantor can, in fact, provide.

3. **Money must be used for what you *and* they want to do.** You may have the best idea in the world for a parent involvement program, but if it does not fit the grantor's philanthropic mission, they won't support it. The secret is to learn what kinds of things the grantor funds and look for ways to capitalize on their objectives to support your own school program. Often, it's not that hard: if you want to promote parent involvement, and the grantor is looking for ways to support technology use in the school, figure out how to use technology to promote parent engagement.

4. **Think small**. Most people know about the big grantors—the U.S. government, huge foundations such as Carnegie or Ford, or giant corporations

such as Microsoft and Apple. The competition for their large grants is ferocious; indeed, many districts, nonprofit organizations, and universities have whole departments devoted to securing grant funds. At the same time, literally millions of dollars go unclaimed every year because grant-seekers neglect smaller foundations, local businesses, or other less notable sources of funds. Also, many large foundations and corporations have funds set aside just for grants to smaller schools. Be sure to read their giving restrictions carefully.

Steps in Finding and Securing Grants

1. **Assess your needs**. What areas of your school need enrichment, building-up, or rejuvenation? Or, what areas have a record of accomplishment that a grantor would find attractive enough to support?

2. **Look for grantors**. Search for grant-makers who might support your initiatives.

3. **Write an inquiry letter**. Many grantors want a brief letter (one page or so) outlining your ideas, how you will implement them, and how much it will cost. This is good to have available for other potential donors as well. If it's allowed, call the program officer to talk about your ideas and get their input.

4. **Be flexible and creative**. Be willing to modify and tweak your initial ideas to fit the grantor's goals and agenda.

5. **Think evaluation first**. Evaluation is critical for grantors. Make sure it covers what you promised to do and uses the metrics they understand and value. That usually means numbers, not anecdotes.

6. **Write a clear, succinct, convincing proposal** *that follows their guidelines*. You may think, "Oh, they'll read a few more pages than their maximum." No, they won't. Get help from a grant-writer and an English teacher. No mistakes allowed!

7. **Don't argue**. If they turn you down, ask if they will give you feedback to improve your next application. Never argue; you'll lose, and you may ruin your chances for another application. If you get the grant, but they want some minor changes, don't argue. If

necessary, explain why you proposed what you did, but be willing to adjust to their needs.

8. **Do what you promised to do**. This is what they agreed to pay for, so make sure you do what you committed to do. If things change, contact the grantor immediately; they are usually pretty understanding and flexible.

9. **Follow the rules**. Make sure you meet all reporting requirements and deadlines. Make yourself a good recipient so that you are favored in future competitions.

10. **Help them help you**. Ask what they need to in order to promote their agenda and their grant programs. Do they need videos of the program in action? Teacher testimonials? If so, offer to provide them. Often, they'll put up extra money for these add-ons.

Looking for Grantors

The first step in looking for grant funds is to look both inside the school and at potential grantors. Look for broad areas of need that you can easily document: achievement, parent involvement, attendance, enrichment, and other clear needs. At the same time, consider potential grantors. Because grant guidelines tend to be pretty broad, it's easier to adapt your program to their goals than it is to try to convince them that they should adapt their goals to your program. The bottom line: they won't.

Thanks to the internet, looking for grants has become much easier than it was even a decade ago. In fact, there are several websites that actually compile information about education grants and give great advice on how to secure them. They even provide sample inquiry letters, grant proposals, reporting forms, and evaluation instruments. Reliable sources include *About School Grants*, *Grants Alert*, and *Get Ed Funding*. Their contact information is located in the Resources section of this chapter.

Community Foundations

In addition to foundations, many state and local governments award grants to schools as well. State grants tend to focus on state standards, priorities, and initiatives, so they are usually aligned very well with the school's agenda and are not likely to disrupt normal programs. Check out your state department of education website for details and current grants, or visit school-grants.org (www.k12grants.org/Grants/state.htm) for links to all state DOE websites.

Local businesses and large corporations with a local presence are a good source of grants for schools as well. Usually, large companies establish foundations that distribute grant funds to local communities or major national projects. A good place to start is by looking at the businesses that are in the school's community, then visiting their website for information about their giving programs. Typically, these are listed under "community affairs," "donations," or "corporate social responsibility" on the company's website. Target stores, a major education donor, showcases their projects under the heading of "corporate responsibility," (https://corporate.target.com/corporate-responsibility#?lnk = fnav_t_spc_1_10). If you can't find grant information on a company's home page, go to the "About" section of the website; it's usually available there.

In addition to individual websites, the Foundation Center (2013b, a) can help schools locate potential funders in their states and communities with the Foundation Directory (http://fconline.foundationcenter.org/). This powerful tool allows grant-seekers to search thousands of foundations and corporate donors by topic, geographic location, amount of funding needed, and a number of other variables. A paid subscription, which can be shared within a school district, provides vast amounts of information about each foundation, but a free version is very helpful in locating potential funders for further investigation.

Both the *Chronicle of Philanthropy* and *Education Week* are weekly publications that frequently feature news about upcoming grants—especially from the U.S. Department of Education and major foundation or corporate initiatives. Together, they are for educators what the *Wall Street Journal* is for business leaders and investors.

The Proposal

Every major foundation or grantor requires some kind of proposal. Some, especially for small businesses or small family foundations, may be quite informal—nothing more than a letter or e-mail describing the project and how the money will be used. However, because of the volume of proposals they receive, most grantors require a proposal that adheres to very strict guidelines, including the maximum number of pages and the presentation format. Rule #1 is *never* deviate from the prescribed format; that will disqualify your application before it is even read. Increasingly, foundations require that applicants use an electronic, online application form that has very strict parameters for submission.

Fortunately, most of the proposal guidelines are very explicit and easy to follow. They also usually provide a "frequently asked questions" (FAQ) section to handle most routine matters. The guidelines and FAQs from Shell Oil Company are pretty typical.

Frequently Asked Questions—Grants

Procedures

No telephoned, faxed, mailed or emailed requests will be considered. To submit a request for consideration, please use our online application form. Due to the volume of requests for donations and sponsorships received, we are unable to respond personally to telephoned, faxed, mailed and emailed inquiries regarding the status of requests.

Contribution Criteria

To be eligible to receive a contribution from Shell, the requesting organization must be designated a 501(c)3 non-profit organization by the US Internal Revenue Service. Generally, the purpose of the organization, event or program must be to provide goods or services for low-income and low-middle income persons in need, and the organization, event or program must benefit persons or communities served by Shell locations.

General Limitations and Exclusions

To maximize the impact of our charitable giving within our budgetary limits, we will limit our contributions to one grant application per organization per fiscal year (September—August), and we will not provide repetitive annual grants or continuing support for organizations or programs. We will review applications from organizations that have received previous support from Shell as new requests and will evaluate the request in relation to other submitted applications and budgetary considerations.

Q. I mailed a letter to Shell. Why didn't I receive a response?

A. Due to the volume of requests for donations and sponsorships received, we are unable to respond personally to telephoned, faxed, mailed and emailed inquiries regarding the status of requests.

Q. My funding request does not fall under any of your programs. How do I submit it?

A. We do not make grants outside our funding priorities.

Q. I am an individual seeking financial assistance. Am I eligible for a grant?

A. In keeping with our charter, we do not provide funding to individuals. We only accept proposals from 501(c)(3) and other tax-exempt organizations.

Q. I have materials I want to submit along with my request for funding. How do I send them?

A. We are not able to accept samples, prototypes, or other supplementary materials that accompany initial requests for funding, and these items will not be returned.

Q. I am raising money for a cause. Am I eligible for a grant?

A. Shell makes grants to organizations directly rather than through individual fundraising activities; therefore, we are unable to fund your effort.

Q. Is there a limit on space for the program overview description?

A. The program overview area will hold 500 words or approximately 3000 characters. This is equivalent to 1 ½ pages of information.

(Shell US, 2014)

The key to successful proposal writing is to align your request with their goals, priorities, and procedures. If Shell says, "the organization, event or program must benefit persons or communities served by Shell locations," that's what they mean. Don't waste your time by trying to convince them that your community is deserving of their support if you do not meet that basic requirement.

The proposal itself is absolutely critical. Consider the fact that yours may be one of thousands they receive. The trick is to make it engaging and interesting without making it look or sound artificial, insincere, or downright goofy.

Help Is Just a Click Away

Fortunately, there are dozens of resources on the internet that can help novice grant-writers craft professional, effective proposals. One of the best is from the Foundation Center (2013b), which offers both free and low-cost resources, including very high-quality instructional videos, on how to write winning proposals. Writing for the NEA, Cynthia McCabe (2007, November) suggests some basic principles for all proposals.

1. **Be Brave!** Don't doubt yourself or your ability to pull off a major project. In other words, don't take yourself out of the running because of self-doubt or fear of failure. The authors of this book—and most other writers and grant-seekers—could paper a wall with the rejection notices they have received, but tenacity is a key ingredient in finding funds. The effort isn't wasted; proposals can sometimes be recycled to other funders or tweaked based on feedback.

2. **Keep the Writing Simple.** You aren't showing off all that you know, you are asking for help to do something exciting. Don't kill that excitement with inflated, academic language. Keeping it simple starts with an abstract and objective. Grantors love a two- or three-sentence summary followed by bullet points of the major elements of the project. Strive for clarity, not page count.

3. **Think Like the Funder.** Consider who is reading the proposal, and stick to their format. Use headings that match the categories of information they are looking for so that the reader can find your key points easily and match them up with their evaluation criteria.

4. **Junk the Jargon.** Let's face it: educationese is pretty awful and doesn't communicate much to most readers. McCabe gives a great example of how to kill a proposal with language. "Nowhere in your grant should the

following sentence appear: 'Using a group of school-age learners, we will endeavor to capitalize on NCLB-specific requirements and shift the paradigm for meeting tangible literary and technological benchmarks.' Reviewers will be much happier to read: 'We want to provide one class of third-graders the equipment needed to produce a book report podcast.'"

5. **Identify Measurable Points and Objectives.** This is the age of accountability, so identify measurable outcomes. "Students will produce a five-minute documentary film on turtles" is better than "students will be exposed to strategies for documentary film making." Be concrete, specific, and, to the extent possible, include quantitative data and evidence.

6. **Bring in Other Disciplines and Technology.** With apologies to John Donne, no subject is an island. Grantors like to see interdisciplinary projects because most believe that is the key to lasting learning and because involving more people increases the bang for their philanthropic bucks. For example, history projects can include science and math (How much feed did it take for Hannibal to get his elephants over the Alps?), and most grantors want to see the innovative use of appropriate technologies to increase student engagement.

7. **Get Help; Build Networks and Partnerships.** Use online resources, local college and university faculty, and district office people to help flesh out the idea and craft a good proposal. Sometimes, this kind of consultation will also produce partnerships—like with a university or local business—that makes the funder much more interested in your proposal. One Connecticut science teacher actually created a virtual network of middle school teachers whose students analyzed drinking water in their local communities. His Facebook and blog postings attracted hundreds of classroom teachers from all over the world, and the grantor loved it so much they doubled the initial amount of the award to more than $200,000!

Grants are a great source of funding to help support the expansion or improvement of school programs. Although school leaders may not be outstanding grant writers themselves, there are several important strategies they can use to make their school "grant competition ready."

● **Create Boilerplate.** "Boilerplate" is the material that most grantors ask for, so schools can save a lot of time by having it ready to go in order to meet a short deadline. Boilerplate usually includes basic information about the school, its community, the staff, the student body, and any special features of the school (Title 1, magnet, alternative, academy model) that may be relevant to the grant request.

- **Build a Team.** Create a grant-writing team that is willing to help conceptualize projects and draft proposals. Include at least one excellent writer, a technology wiz, a representative from the leadership team, and perhaps a parent or community member. You can add subject specialists as needed for specific grant applications, and don't overlook community members who might have grant writing experience. (One of the ways the authors "volunteer" in their community schools is by helping schools write grant proposals and find partners in their own or other communities.)

- **Maintain an Idea File.** Ask teachers, students, parents, and community members to give you ideas that might be turned into grant applications. You might even create an online form that asks for a description of the idea, who would be involved, how it would work in the school, and how much money is needed. Stored electronically, these not only become a good resource for grant applications, but they get people thinking about grants as a normal part of the school's operations.

- **Think Sustainability.** No matter how great your idea is, funders always have one question in mind: "how will this program or project be continued once our funding ends?" When thinking about potential projects, consider the changes that will have to be made in the school in order to sustain the program or major portions of it when the grant funding cycle ends. Better yet, plan for how the program can be "scaled up" across your district, community, or state.

- **Create Grant Finding Routines.** Put together a list of websites or other resources that you scan on a weekly basis for new grant announcements and opportunities. Use some of the sites in the Resources section of this chapter or locate and compile your own. A Colorado high school has students scan identified sites for grant opportunities as part of their service requirement. Beyond the sites selected by the administration, students will actually search for and fill "custom orders" for teachers who are looking for support for specific programs or content areas.

Grants are big business and there is a lot of competition. However, good projects that are clearly stated and carefully planned are very attractive to funders—especially in local communities. Also, even the big foundations are impressed by "grass roots" applications from real teachers and administrators working in real schools. It may be helpful to have an experienced partner, but most funders would rather support the honest and sincere application that comes from a school or district than one that comes from a "grant factory." Take a chance on a grant—even a small one. The investment is small and the payoff may be huge.

Contracts

Contracts differ from grants in one major way: they are legally enforceable agreements that usually have penalties for non-performance. A school may disappoint a grant-maker, and may even have to return funds, but violating a contract is usually a major problem that attracts mostly unwanted attention, legal action, extra costs, and long-term organizational consequences. For that reason, districts have very specific rules for entering into contracts and individual school leaders rarely have the authority to do so on their own.

But that doesn't mean that individual leaders can't look for contractual opportunities that may produce revenue for the school and comply with district policies. Most contracts between schools and the outside world involve three kinds of activity—(1) exclusive purchase agreements, (2) renting and leasing school property, or (3) providing services on a contracted basis for outside agencies.

Exclusive purchase agreements occur when a school agrees to use a specific product or vendor in exchange for some kind of premium or pay back. As discussed in Chapter 8, these are often considered sponsorships or partnerships in which a school may use a specific soft drink vendor in exchange for a building improvement, such as a new scoreboard for the gym, or an actual cash payment for placement of vending machines or products in the cafeteria.

Renting and leasing of school facilities is much more common, and many school buildings are used during their off hours by churches, colleges, community centers and agencies, or other groups. In one case in New York State, the district leases an elementary school to a private nonprofit agency that offers summer computer game design "camps" for area students. In

Florida, athletic fields are used by community groups for a softball league, and a Minnesota district rents its hockey rink to the community recreation center for their own hockey competition. One Texas high school even leases its roof to a billboard company to market products to travelers flying in to Houston Intercontinental Airport.

Other lease arrangements are starting to emerge and may, in fact, be quite controversial. One large Florida district leased unused district land, some of it adjoining school athletic fields, for the placement of cell phone towers. These long-term leases generated a substantial amount of money and no shortage of public concern. The controversy stems from the debate that still rages about the effects of radio waves—a form of electromagnetic radiation—on human health. Some scientists claim it can be harmful; others say that low levels of this radiation are a normal part of our environment and are no more harmful than a computer screen or TV set.

Because the payoff is quite high, many districts have moved ahead with cell tower placements even in the face of some push back by the public. In Hillsborough County (FL) citizens objected to cell tower placement because of the size of the towers and violation of the setback rules in largely residential neighborhoods. In Georgia, a bill has been introduced in the legislature to prohibit construction of all cell towers on school grounds in the state, and dozens of individual school districts from Massachusetts to Oregon have banned them as well. Other districts have continued to lease space for the towers and have made accommodations to public concern. Anne Arundel County (MD) hopes to erect 40 towers on school property that will generate more than $5 million by 2021. Nearby, Montgomery County (MD) realizes almost $900,000 a year from cell tower leases, but allows parents to vote on the placement of towers on individual school grounds.

Providing services is somewhat trickier than contracts because it involves both employment law and, in some communities, either informal or formal "non-compete" agreements with local businesses. Savvy school leaders hardly want to put themselves in the position of competing with a local business that provides essentially the same service as the school might supply. But sometimes it can be made to work to everyone's satisfaction.

In a large Midwestern city, a local computer vendor used both school facilities and instructors to provide basic instruction for people who purchased their products. Instead of traveling to the city center to get training, buyers could attend sessions at a school in their neighborhood. In New Jersey, an immigrant placement and assistance center used local schools to provide English language instruction and cultural coaching for newcomers from Southeast Asia, Latin America, Russia, and Africa. The center contracted with the district, which, in turn, hired certified teachers at their hourly rate. In Oregon, a public charter school provides specialized instructional resources—on a fee-for-service basis—for parents who home-school their children. These students may participate in extracurricular activities, receive music lessons, obtain tutoring help, or even have in-home proctors manage exams for on-line courses they may be taking from a remote provider. In this particular case, the principal consulted with his faculty to identify the kinds of services that might be provided and how to price them fairly to encourage participation and still compensate the school and the staff for extra work.

One of the biggest issues in providing services is deciding where the boundary is between normal services a school should provide and extra services that might become fee-based. Is helping kids get ready for college placement tests a routine obligation of the school or should parents pay for that extra help just as they might through a private vendor? How about tutoring? Is that an obligation of the school, or is it an extra service that families need to purchase? Are individual music lessons part of the curriculum or should they be available for an extra charge? In the New Normal environment, school leaders will continue to struggle with these and other sticky issues in order to strike a balance between revenue generation and equitable education for every child.

Entrepreneurial Activity

Outside of the relatively normal approaches outlined above, some schools have ventured fully into entrepreneurial activity designed to (1) give kids experiences with building and managing a business and (2) make money. These kinds of activities normally fall into three categories:

1. Retail operations housed completely within the school
2. Services and products available to both students and the public
3. Creation of products for sale outside of the school

Retail operations are fairly common in many schools. Most of the activities are pretty small and rather conventional. Many schools have a school store that sells supplies, spirit wear, limited health/beauty products, and snacks. Most of these are managed by students working under faculty supervision, and the proceeds go to student activities, scholarships, and other purchases that benefit the students pretty directly.

Services and products available to both students and the public are still usually focused on school-related events. Food and beverage sales at athletic events, musical shows, or school plays are usually student-run and may benefit a specific group—such as athletic boosters or band parents. These kinds of activities have been going on for a long time and are usually regulated by district policy or even state law.

Recently, some schools have invested in creating coffee bars or coffee and specialty beverage carts that are available to students, faculty, and school visitors. Capitalizing on the popularity of coffee shops and the vast variety of coffee and tea products now available, these aromatic and highly profitable cafés are run by student baristas under the direction of a faculty advisor. In some schools, students who have free periods are allowed to patronize the coffee shop and visit with their friends; in others, the venue is open only during specific hours. In still other schools, students (and teachers) are free to bring drinks purchased in the school's coffee shop to class. Some even serve pastries made either by the cafeteria staff (working overtime) or by outside vendors. In at least one small western town, the school's local coffee shop is the only specialty coffee vendor in town, so it does a brisk business among local townspeople on their way to work.

In several Oregon schools, a local foundation provided the funds to set up the coffee business. They provided equipment, initial inventory, and some business consulting services to help arrange the financial management system and conduct research on starting a business in a school. Principals and staff laud the program, and the coffee shops generate both substantial revenue and great entrepreneurial experience for the students.

Products for sale comprise a fairly new and growing category of revenue generators for schools. Just as in the real world of business, some are remarkable for their success; others never really fulfill the promise of what seemed to be a good idea at the time. Four examples illustrate the diversity of these projects.

● In New York, a regional vocational high school provides **auto body repair** for the cost of materials and a fee. The work is supervised by a professional auto body repair person, who is also the teacher, and is generally of very good quality. Most people wouldn't bring their Porsche or Rolls Royce to the high school for body work, but a lot of students and their families get basic repairs done at a reasonable cost—at the same time the students have an opportunity to work on real problems and repair scenarios.

● Homeowners near this Indianapolis suburb can purchase **garden sheds** and other small outbuildings constructed by student volunteers and those enrolled in a basic construction course at the local high school. Limited styles allow for economical material purchases and construction, and the designs are compatible with the Midwestern architecture of the town. Deliveries are made by a professional moving company, so insurance issues are reduced. Recently, the school has begun to contract with a local garden center to feature the sheds in their retail facility.

● Florida art lovers can purchase **student art works** at a twice-yearly show hosted at the school and in a number of local businesses (mostly restaurants and coffee shops) that display student art throughout the year. A portion of the sale price goes to the student artist and a portion is retained by the school for art supplies and program costs. One student piece was purchased by a nonprofit environmental group who then also bought the rights to use the art work on T-shirts and reusable shopping bags now seen all over town.

● **Food, Fish, Honey, and Bikes** are all produced at Al Kennedy High School in Cottage Grove, Oregon. This remarkable alternative school with a commitment to sustainability partners with a bike manufacturer to produce bicycle frames, maintains an organic garden that supplies local restaurants, food banks, their own produce stand, and the school cafeteria (more than 5 tons in the past few years), a beekeeping area that provides hundreds of pounds of saleable honey, and an tilapia farm that raises organic fish for food banks and local sales. Students are involved in every aspect of these operations, with the result that they remain deeply engaged in the school's "real world" program and gain invaluable experience in creating and managing sustainable businesses.

In every case, these successful programs grow out of the school's fundamental mission—to provide hands-on, real world experiences for students who will have to function in the entrepreneurial, globally competitive world they will inhabit as adults.

The Relief of Change

There is a certain relief in change, even though it be from bad to worse; as I have found in traveling in a stagecoach, that it often a comfort to shift one's position and be bruised in a new place.

Washington Irving

Becoming an Edupreneur

Turning educational activity into a profitable venture is not part of the training that any of us raised in the tradition of Horace Mann ever received. But despite the uneasiness that many of us may feel about this kind of venture, there is something very authentic and instructive about it for the students we teach. It would be wonderful if schools had all of the money they needed and didn't have to worry about raising funds. But those days are probably gone—if they ever existed at all. What the New Normal requires of all of us is that we do our best, most creative thinking to preserve the most important parts of our school's mission, let go of the things that are no longer essential or cost-effective, and reinvent the way in which we provide high-quality, sustainable educational services for all of our children and youth.

Think About It

Becoming an Edupreneur

1. Make a list of "saleable" items or services you believe might boost school revenue and help pay for specific programs or activities. What kinds of products come from normal academic processes that might be attractive to people outside the school?

2. Who (or which partners or businesses) might be interested in a partnership that might produce revenue for the school? How should you approach them?

Now Try This

1. Ask your faculty and staff to think about ways they think the school can raise revenue through entrepreneurial activity. Use some of the examples in this chapter to stimulate conversation. Begin with e-mails or written suggestions.

2. Call other principals you know to see if they have revenue-generating activities that work in their schools.

3. Compile the suggestions and use them as a basis for a conversation at a faculty meeting. Identify the most promising ideas (and the least complicated ones) to begin.

4. Brainstorm possible sources for "start up" funds and productive partnerships.

5. Solicit a group of volunteers to do some preliminary planning on the best ideas.

Grant Resources

- National Education Association Foundation
  www.neafoundation.org/pages/grants-to-educators/
- Grantsalert.com
  www.grantsalert.com/
- GetEdFunding.com
  www.getedfunding.com
- About School Grants
  www.k12grants.org/about.htm

IV Tools and Strategies

We've both been school leaders. We understand the complexity of the role, and we talk often about the different strategies and tools we used when we were principals. We believe strongly in the importance, even in a time of declining resources, of providing every student with access to the very best educational experience. Part IV is designed to suggest a whole set of tools that you can add to your toolbox. We recognize that every tool doesn't fit every situation. That's why leaders always want to have a toolbox stuffed with ideas. We hope these tools help you insure that your school provides students with those good educational experiences they need.

10 | Leadership Tools and Strategies

Schools are under tremendous pressure to change the educational experience of their students in response to internal needs and continued pressure of external groups such as state legislatures, foundations, and advocacy groups. One of the realities of the current environment is that schools are asked to get different and better results while dealing with stable or declining resources.

Most organizations, such as schools, resist change. In fact, educators are adept at resistance. We question the motivation of the legislature, advocacy groups, or parents, and we suggest that if we only had more resources we could make the needed improvements.

Despite this bleak description, many school leaders recognize the need to challenge the status quo and the behaviors that cling to past practice failing to recognize this new reality. A few years ago Ron worked with a Tucson high school principal. She described her arrival as "lots of good people trying to do things that made a difference." But she recognized that there was a campus-wide climate of distrust and cynicism. Every project operated independently with little coordination. Things needed to change.

This chapter will share strategies and tools that school leaders can use to work with teachers and community to respond to the reality of limited resources. We'll share ideas that we've gathered from principals we've worked with in all sections of the country. From these principals we've learned about ways to build trust, display confidence, and promote optimism about the future.

The North Central Regional Educational Lab (Walter, 2004) identified several key characteristics of successful improvement initiatives. Those characteristics include:

- A clear, compelling, and collectively held vision and institutional mission
- An engaged, involved, and committed professional community
- An unrelenting focus on improved learning for students
- The presence of sustained, focused professional learning
- Creation and nurturance of partnerships with families and community

The remainder of this section will discuss these characteristics and identify strategies and tools that school leaders can use to successfully navigate the new reality of declining resources.

Getting Started

Recognizing the need to make changes is just the first step, but when it deals with the allocation and use of resources the work can be particularly daunting. Change that is mandated or externally driven almost always provokes resistance. But change that emerges from a thoughtful and collaborative process is more likely to be successful. Throughout this book we've shared examples of ways principals worked with their staff and community to modify their program when faced with declining resources. Almost always they used an engaging and collaborative process.

What's clear is that successful planning is collaborative, anchored in a shared vision, driven by data and other forms of information, and transparent and open.

Importance of a Clear Vision

The most successful improvement plans are characterized by a clear, collectively held vision and institutional mission. The vision becomes the litmus test for every new or refined program and practice.

When we work with schools, we find that the most successful have a clear, compelling vision. Almost always the vision was one developed with teachers, staff, and families, but it was shaped by the vision of the principal. More importantly, once the vision was developed it became a living statement that was used to measure the value and importance of every school activity. Programs and practices that did not align with the vision and mission were modified or abandoned, and new programs were only adopted when they advanced the mission.

A newly appointed high school principal in west Texas recognized the need to improve student achievement, particularly for the school's minority students. She said, "The school, while good, wasn't getting the results we needed for many students. Good wasn't good enough. We had to refocus and make a commitment to every student's success."

At the same time the west Texas oil industry was struggling with the economic downturn and resources for schools were tight. The district made it clear there would be no additional funds. In fact, the principal was directed to find ways to reduce her budget.

Undaunted, the principal organized a group of teachers and other staff to review their school's vision and update it so that it aligned with current needs. The result was a simple statement—"We, the faculty of the Senior High School, believe that our primary purposes are teaching and learning." Straightforward and direct, the vision, once agreed upon became the measure of which programs remained, which changed, and which ended.

The challenge with any vision or mission statement is in its implementation. Data about student learning at the school clearly indicated that many students were not doing well in mathematics. While many students were challenged and very successful, many others were underserved by the current offerings and instructional approach. The principal was direct with her staff about the need for change. This led nearly every member of the mathematics department to transfer, retire, or leave the school.

Undaunted, the principal enthusiastically launched a search for teachers. Rather than retreat from the school's mission, she saw the staff changes as an opportunity to recruit and hire faculty who shared her vision for the school and were committed to ensuring the academic success of every student, regardless of ability or background. New courses were created and replaced remedial options. Extra time was added to the schedule to extend math classes. New instructional practices and added technology was infused throughout the program. Scores continue to rise, all without adding programs, increasing staff or other resources.

At a Tacoma (WA) high school a new principal arrived with a steadfast commitment to changing the culture of his school. He was troubled by the prevalence of traditional teacher-centered instruction and the tendency to blame students, and their families, for student learning problems. The Tacoma Public Schools, like virtually every school district in the nation, had limited resources to pay for a comprehensive professional development program. So the principal worked closely with several Seattle area foundations to secure the funds to train every teacher in the techniques used by Advanced Placement teachers. Classes become more engaging and more rigorous, and test scores and college admission, improved.

Across the continent, a middle school principal in the Rockaway Beach area of New York City was concerned about his school's connections to the community it served. The school looked like a fortress—locked doors, metal detectors at entrances, police patrolling the exterior. This principal would not accept this reality for his school. With few resources he used his personal relationship with parents and community to organize, nurture, and sustain a community group dedicated to changing the image of the school.

A remarkable transformation occurred. The school became a community center hosting a variety of school and community events. It was a busy, vibrant place during the school day and well into the evening. Staff morale improved, student absenteeism declined, test scores rose. One student remarked, "Mr. D really cares about us. I feel really safe here and able to focus on my studies."

Each of these principals had a vision for their students and their school. They acted on that vision, despite the lack of additional resources, to overcome barriers that were accepted by leaders in other schools. Their commitment, their drive, and their willingness to see opportunity where others saw barriers, truly transformed their schools.

Your Personal Vision

The frantic life of a principal rarely provides time to step back and reflect on those beliefs that shape and guide your personal and professional life. Yet being clear about those personal beliefs that shape your work and relationships with people is essential.

Taking time to stop, reflect, and identify those things that contribute to your personal vision for your school is critical. Often this introspective process leads to a recommitment to the core values that led you to become a principal in the first place.

Preparing a written statement of personal vision provides an opportunity to think about the words you use, to consider their nuances, and to grapple with balancing multiple values and priorities. One principal we worked with described writing a vision statement as "the most challenging thing I ever wrote. But also the most valuable."

A four-step process for thinking about your personal vision includes reflecting on your own personal and professional life, identifying those things of greatest value, and using these insights to write a personal vision.

Process for Developing a Personal Vision Statement

Step 1: Think about your personal and professional life. Make a list of what you would like to achieve and the contributions you would like to make. Describe what it looks like and feels like. For example, hovering in a hot air balloon over your life, imagine it as successful as it might be—what would you see, what would you feel, what would you hear?

Step 2: Consider the following things about what you have written—relationships, personal interests, and community. Examine each item in your list to ensure that it still fits.

Step 3: Develop a list of values. Identify the most important values in your life. Once this is done, review the list and rank them from most to least important. Remove the least important. Re-rank if appropriate. Check for relevance with your earlier list. Eliminate any item that is not relevant.

Step 4: Use the items from the first three steps to develop a statement of personal vision. Review and edit the statement as often as needed until you believe it accurately reflects who you are and what you want to be.

Adapted from: Williamson and Blackburn's *The Principalship from A to Z* (2009).

Developing your own personal vision is not easy. Because a vision reflects our core beliefs about our work and our lives, preparing a statement of personal vision can be challenging; however, work on a personal vision, or ethic, has been described as one of the most important things a leader can do. It helps one to become clearer about what they value and about what is most important in their school.

Creating or Recommitting to a School-Wide Vision

Successful principals recognize the importance of working with their school community to develop, nurture, and sustain a collectively held vision for their school.

Every school we visit has a mission or vision statement. Many, however, are out-of-date and rarely used to set goals and priorities, allocation of resources, or make decisions about school programs. Even the clearest statements need periodic review. A review allows you to adjust the mission and vision based on up-to-date information about students and their needs. A review also allows the staff "to recommit to the school's core values and beliefs" (Williamson & Blackburn, 2009).

Process for Developing a School Vision Statement

Activity 1: What are the things people are pleased with and frustrated about at this school? (Designed to get the issues on the table.)

Activity 2: Invite the group to consider the values that should guide the school. You might ask, "As we begin planning for our future, what values are most important to you as we create our vision statement?" (Use of "I believe" statements focus on the important things.)

Note: A helpful approach is to have the group read some common things. For example, information about developmental needs of students, future trends, information about recommendations for schools at that level. Often professional associations (NASSP, ASCD) have useful resources. Shared readings create a common base of information and are particularly useful to minimize the barriers between teachers and parents where parents often defer to teachers as the "experts."

Activity 3: Ask the group to respond to the following. "Imagine it is five years from today. We have been able to operationalize our beliefs. What does our school look, sound and feel like? Describe the vision." (Helps to identify the target the school will work towards.)

Activity 4: In work groups, develop a draft mission statement to be shared with the larger group. (Development of multiple models promotes discussion, clarification, and consensus building).

Activity 5: Share the drafts, ask questions and seek clarification, and seek consensus on a statement. Plan to share it with the larger school community for feedback and comment.

From: Williamson and Blackburn's *The Principalship from A to Z* (2009).

Vision is one of the most important components of an effective school. Being clear about your personal vision, and working with others to be clear about the vision for your school, helps you and your faculty balance competing demands and make decisions based on your collective vision for your school.

Creating Professional Community

Formal and informal collaborative groups characterize successful schools. Principals recognize that ensuring the success of every student requires less emphasis on individual work and greater reliance on the power of organizational collaboration.

Many principals tap into long-standing groups such as content area departments and School Improvement Teams. Others are comfortable establishing fluid and dynamic work groups focused on a specific task.

Most importantly, successful principals recognize that their schools are better, and get better results, when they move beyond a primary focus on developing the knowledge and skills of individual teachers to building the collective capacity for the organization. These schools are characterized by the creation of intentional groups that transcend traditional school groups.

At a San Antonio high school, the principal recognized the need to re-commit her staff to students and their learning. This large urban school had few resources to add programs and services. The principal understood that even without additional resources she could reorganize her school, modify the schedule, and find ways for teaches to work with one another.

After months of discussion the staff agreed to reorganize the school into four, semi-autonomous learning communities. Each community is responsible for the primary instruction of a group of students and responsible for monitoring student success, using common assessments and work samples adjusting their instruction to improve student learning. Teachers share the same students, have a similar schedule, and meet several times each week to talk about student needs and instructional practices. The principal reported that "since we moved to these small groups there has been a clearer commitment to the success of every student. We continue to improve and to develop the skills to work with one another. It's amazing what we can learn from one another about good teaching."

The work groups at this school were intentionally focused on professional conversation about teaching and instructional practice. One teacher described this emphasis as the "single action that transformed us from a collection of individuals to a group committed to improving student learning."

In southeastern Arizona the principal of a rural high school knew that ninth grade was a pivotal year for many students. Ninth grade was when many students decided to leave school. Midway through his first year as principal he began to meet with teachers who worked primarily with ninth graders. They discussed their curricula, shared instructional strategies, and worked on developing a consistent approach to classroom management, assignment of homework, and instruction. Without any additional resources for materials or staff, the collaborative conversations at this school led to more interdisciplinary links between subjects and a more consistent and coherent program for ninth graders. Most importantly, the number of students dropping out of school declined.

Professional Learning

Valuing professional learning is important but it is essential that opportunities for authentic professional learning be provided for all teachers and other staff. There are lots of ways to promote professional learning including organizing into professional learning communities (PLCs), designing a schedule that includes time for common planning, redesigning the use of faculty meetings, and refocusing professional development.

The term *professional learning community* is used to describe many collaborative activities but the "professional community of learners" originally described by Astuto et al. (1993) and then promoted by DeFour (2010) reflects a deep commitment of teachers and leaders to learning and growing professionally, and then using their learning to improve student learning.

We value the power of a PLC to change professional learning in a school and recognize that there are lots of ways to promote professional learning. One way is to abandon traditional forms of professional development, activities that often occur in large groups and have little relevance to the actual work of teachers. In their place many schools are organizing book study groups, having teams of teachers look at student work, conducting learning walks around the school, or participating in a lesson study.

Selecting a Strategy

Strategy	How this strategy could impact student learning
Book Study: Select a book that everyone will read and have conversations about the content and how it can impact student learning.	
Look at Student Work: Organize teams of teachers (content or grade level) to look at samples of student work to align expectations and promote quality (www.lasw.org).	
Learning Walks: Similar to walkthroughs, organize learning walks led by teachers and designed to gather data about instructional practices.	
Lesson Study: Small groups of teachers work together to design, teach, and refine a lesson as a way to improve student learning (www.tc.edu/lessonstudy/lessonstudy.html).	
Instructional Rounds: Organized like rounds among medical interns, teachers, and leaders visit classrooms to observe teachers and identify ways to improve teaching. Rounds are followed by self-reflection and discussion. (www.hepg.org/hel/article/157) .	

The principal of a large, comprehensive high school outside of Houston worked with his School Improvement Team to organize book study groups among his staff. Every teacher belonged to a book study group. The books varied among groups, and were selected by the group. The staff of the Model Schools Consortium recommended most books used by the groups. Because there were no additional funds to purchase books, the principal worked with his parent advisory board to identify local businesses that were willing to donate funds to purchase books for staff to read. Teachers used time during team and content meetings to discuss the books, share their learning and talk about how they could use this learning to improve the school. One staff meeting each month was devoted to the book study effort. Over the course of a year, the commitment to learning and growing together, transformed the climate at his school.

At a rural Oregon middle school, a principal and his leadership team participated in regional training on the lesson study model. They returned to school enthusiastic about how the approach could strengthen instruction and impact student learning. Their school was located in a small, poor, rural community that was supportive of its schools but unable to provide additional funds to support the training needed to implement the model.

Upon learning that the training would be available in a larger community nearby, the principal encouraged teacher participation and juggled assignments and his limited budget to cover the costs. Several teachers attended and returned to school where they organized an interdisciplinary group to implement the lesson study design. They chose a content area, designed a lesson, selected one member to teach the lesson while others observed, and then debriefed and redesigned the lesson based on their observation. The experience allowed teachers to become more familiar with the content of other subjects and to build a trusting, collegial climate where professional learning was valued.

Decision-Making Tools

Throughout the book we've shared tools that school leaders can use to facilitate discussions about dealing with declining resources. When working with groups, you want to have clarity about the task and how decisions will be made. You also want to use strategies and tools that promote thoughtful and reflective discussion, rather than limiting or inhibiting debate.

Here are several tools that we've found helpful when we work with groups. Each is designed to engage participants in the discussion and examination of issues. Like any collection of tools, not every tool fits every situation, and leaders will want to choose the tool that will be most helpful.

Nominal Group Technique

The Nominal Group Technique is often used to generate lots of ideas and to allow people to participate freely. It can also be used to identify priorities or select alternatives for further discussion.

Nominal Group Process

- Seat participants in small groups to promote discussion and interaction.
- Share a focus question to guide the discussion, assuring participants there is no "right" answer.
- Allow participants to silently reflect, brainstorm ideas, and write them on paper.
- Do a round robin sharing of ideas until all ideas are shared. Record ideas on chart paper. Don't combine similar ideas at this time.
- Discuss and clarify all ideas.
- Rank alternatives and then discuss each alternative.
- Ask each participant to rank the alternatives. Rankings are averaged.
- Participants review rankings and discuss results.

Plus/Delta—The Plus/Delta tool is designed to identify things that are working (Plus) and opportunities for improvement (Delta). Many facilitators use the Plus/Delta to identify areas for further discussion.

+	Δ

The Plus/Delta tool is helpful to launch a discussion or to debrief a meeting or activity.

Upside, Onside, Downside

This collaborative tool is a variation of the Plus/Delta technique and allows individuals to identify the positive and the things that need attention. The "onside" section of the tool allows participants to identify what they are already doing on an issue. It's another way to engage participants in an analysis of an issue.

↑	**Upside** What are the positives about collaboration?
→	**Onside** What have I already done on collaboration?
↓	**Downside** What are the negatives about collaboration?

SWOT Analysis

A SWOT analysis is used to understand decisions and their implications. SWOT is an acronym for strengths, weaknesses, opportunities, and threats. It provides a framework for a thoughtful analysis of a decision or proposed solution, like reprioritizing a budget.

Strengths	Weaknesses
Opportunities	**Threats**

Strengths and Weaknesses are generally seen as internal to the school or district and are things that tend to be currently present in the organization, things like employees and their skills, adaptability, and infrastructure.

Opportunities and Threats are from the outside, or external, environment. They may be factors that like competition, technological changes, or legal challenges.

Force Field Analysis

A Force Field Analysis is a tool for diagnosing issues, and it provides clear guidance about action. The process works well with small as well as large groups and provides an opportunity to examine both facilitators and inhibitors of change.

Driving Forces—Driving forces are those forces affecting a situation that are pushing in a particular direction. They tend to initiate a change and keep it going. Examples might include data about student learning, demographic data, or economic trends.

Restraining Forces—Restraining forces are forces that act to restrain or decrease the driving forces. Examples might include apathy, contractual issues, or costs.

Where a plan has been decided on, a Force Field Analysis allows you to look at all the forces that either support or work against the plan. It helps you to plan or reduce the impact of the opposing forces, and strengthen and reinforce the supporting forces.

Conducting a Force Field Analysis—When you conduct a Force Field Analysis, first state the issue. Then identify the factors working for and against the issue. Discuss the strength of each factor and rank them. This helps identify steps you might take to minimize the factors working against the plan.

Description of Issue:	
Factors Working For	Factors Working Against

Next Steps:	

Force Field Analysis is a useful method for analyzing the forces for and against an innovation. It helps you identify the potential success of a plan, assess whether a plan is worth pursuing, identify changes that might improve the plan, and identify appropriate next steps.

Quadrant Process

The Quadrant Process is useful to analyze issues so that you can assess the resistance that might be present. It allows you to visually demonstrate the high/ low or positive/negative relationship between factors impacting a decision.

Create the quadrants on chart paper and post it in the meeting room. As you discuss issues, ask the group to identify where they appropriately belong based on the impact and potential resistance.

High Impact	
Low	High
Resistance	Resistance
Low Impact	

Decision-Making Tools

In Chapter 7, we discussed ways to work with stakeholders to do things like reprioritizing your budget. We discussed consensus and several other ways to make decisions. We won't repeat that information but want to remind you of those strategies and tools.

Decision-Making Strategies

- Absolute Consensus
- All but Two
- Multi-Voting
- Super-Majority
- Simple Majority
- Fist to Five

Now Try This

Consider the collaborative tools describe in this chapter. Describe how you might use one or two of them to engage stakeholders in a discussion about reprioritizing the budget.

_____
_____
_____
_____
_____
_____
_____
_____

Successful School-Family-Community Partnerships

Successful principals recognize the important role that families play in supporting the school's academic mission. They value family involvement in their school's program, and are particularly attentive to building relationships with families that traditionally are not involved in school life.

When resources are limited, or declining, there's a tendency to believe that new programs can't be launched. That's often not the case, and we'd like to share two examples of principals who recognized a need and found ways to respond to those needs without using additional staff or resources.

The principal of a large urban high school in Houston knew that some of his students left school early each afternoon. Rather than focusing solely on truancy, he was concerned that, as a result of non-attendance, students would fail classes and drop out of school. When he investigated the reasons for departing, he found that nearly all were going to work because their family relied on their income. Armed with this knowledge, the principal worked staff to redesign the school day, extending it on both ends, so that students could start school early in the day, as early as 7 a.m., and then go to work.

Building supportive relationships with all parents characterized the work of the principal of MS #53 in New York City. His school served a diverse community with many upper middle class families as well as families of limited means. Many students from less affluent neighborhoods were bused to his school, and their parents were generally less involved in school life. Rather than accepting the limited involvement, the principal held a series of meetings in community centers in each of his school's neighborhoods. The first round of meetings had sporadic attendance but he persisted. Over time, going into the community built a positive reputation with some of his school's most reluctant parents. The principal invited other staff to attend the sessions and meet parents. Progress was slow but after five years these neighborhood meetings have become one of the defining characteristics of MS #53.

Strengthening Family Engagement

The evidence is clear. All families want to be involved in their child's education. But the level of engagement often varies significantly from community to community. Often a school's family engagement plans are limited to communication from the school to home or to asking families to donate goods and services. The National Network of Partnership Schools (www.csos.jhu.edu) and the Harvard Family Research Project (www.hfrp.org) have studied successful school-family partnerships and find a more inclusive model works best, one that welcomes all parents and provides opportunities for families to be authentically involved in school activities and decision making.

Families and community can be important resources to a school. Often members of the community have knowledge and expertise that can be tapped to strengthen school activities. Families and community members are often able to mobilize a community to provide resources that may be limited. Regardless of the role, when families and community are welcomed and actively engaged in schools, the shared vision for improving the education of students is strengthened.

We've looked at the work of the National Network of Partnership Schools and the Harvard Family Research Project and identified six strategies that can promote healthy school-family-community partnerships.

1. **Check Assumptions and Stereotypes**—Be careful about assumptions and stereotypes about families. Most teachers and other school employees share a middle-class background and view the role of parents through their own experience. Recognize that a diverse parent community reflects a variety of values, beliefs about the role of parents and their relationship to school, and comfort levels in interacting with school personnel. Often minority and poor families feel unwanted and unwelcome in their child's school. Be cautious about relying on training, books, and other resources that make generalizations about poor families or families of diverse cultures. Do not organize your parent engagement program around majority, middle-class norms and values. A single approach to parent engagement will not succeed with all parents.

2. **Build Trusting Relationships**—Personal relationships are important when working with families. Many parents are more comfortable interacting with school personnel in smaller, more intimate settings where it may be possible to share information and ask questions. Latino parents are often concerned about being dismissed due to language or cultural barriers. They are aware of the stereotypes present among school employees, and other parents, and may resist participating in parent activities where those stereotypes may be apparent. Identify ways to meet and talk with families at churches or community centers off campus. Your outreach must be culturally sensitive and specific to each cultural group. Similarly, parents of limited means share these concerns and resist participating

in programs where involvement is measured by the economic resources you can contribute to the school.

3. **Value Robust Two-Way Communication**—All parents want to be active partners in their children's education. An important part of parent engagement is their sense of efficacy, believing that they can contribute to their child's education. It is important to both learn about children from families as well as share information about their children's schooling with their families. Too often school communication is just one way, school to family and just about problems rather than successes. Parents, particularly parents of limited means, but also parents from diverse cultures, perceive that the school may not value their knowledge about their own child. They may resist sharing information that reinforces assumptions they believe school employees hold about their family and their child. Too often schools create structures for parents to share information, but those systems are built on middle-class norms about when and how to interact with the school.

4. **Identify Authentic Opportunities to Learn From Families**—Just as two-way communication is essential, so is creating opportunities for all families to share their knowledge and skills. Parents enjoy the opportunity to contribute their knowledge to the school's program. Don't rely on a parental engagement program based solely on fund-raising or other resource-based programs. Many parents are eager for an opportunity to provide leadership. Seek opportunities for minority parents and parents of limited means to participate in decision-making groups. That may require working with community leaders to identify parents comfortable with that role.

5. **Train Teachers and Other Staff**—It's important to work with teachers and other staff to become knowledgeable about the diverse parent community in your school. The most effective learning occurs when parents representing all parts of your school community participate in the training. Their involvement makes the training more authentic and signals the community that you are committed to learning about and respecting the diversity present in your school. As stated earlier, do not rely on a single book or training session to form generalizations about families.

6. **Develop and Implement a Plan**—Improving parent engagement requires an intentional plan of action. Good intentions are noble but a systematic,

sustained commitment requires planning and resource allocation. The best plans are developed with parents and community. Current governance structures like the School Improvement Team or the PTO may not adequately reflect the diversity of points of view central to a successful plan. Ensure that your planning team is diverse and involves each group that will be part of the plan.

Final Thoughts

The most successful principals have a whole set of strategies and tools they can use to collaborate with teachers, families, and community. They recognize the importance of involving stakeholders when faced with strategic decisions about the future of their school, and they value the perspectives and ideas that stakeholders bring to the discussion. This section provides several tools that leaders can use to ensure that decisions about their school are made in a thoughtful, engaging, and collaborative way.

Resources

Thinking Collaborative—Adaptive Schools Project

www.thinkingcollaborative.com/
This site provides information about the Seven Norms of Collaboration and other collaborative tools. It includes several self-assessment tools.

Seeing Is Believing: Promising Practices for Promoting Family Engagement

(Westmoreland, Rosenberg, Lopez & Weiss, 2009)
http://tinyurl.com/qa9yzw8
This report describes an approach to family engagement using district-wide strategies, building capacity and reaching out to all families. It provides brief vignettes about proven practices.

The Evaluation Exchange: Beyond the Bake Sale: How School Districts Can Promote Family Involvement

http://tinyurl.com/3r2qvwd

This article, adapted from the book *Beyond the Bake Sale* (Henderson, Mapp, Johnson, & Davies, 2007), discusses how districts can create a culture that supports high levels of family engagement.

Walking the Walk: Portraits of Leadership for Family Engagement in Urban Schools

www.eric.ed.gov/PDFS/EJ847415.pdf

This article, while anchored in urban settings, provides useful examples of strategies for building relationships with families of limited means in diverse communities.

Technology Tools

At the same time that schools wrestle with declining resources, a whole set of technology tools have become available that can be used to improve communication, increase productivity, and contribute to professional learning.

Tools to Enhance Communication

One of the fastest growing trends over the last decade has been the growth in social networking. While often considered a tool of the young, a recent Pew study (Lenhart, Purcell, Smitth & Zickuhr, 2010) found that 75% of adults have a presence on one or more social networking sites.

Social Media—For many school leaders social media has become an important tool for communicating with families and community. It is a low-cost tool for sharing information about school events, introducing school staff, providing reminders about school events and promoting your school's success. It is common for a school to have a presence on both Facebook (www.facebook.com) and Twitter (www.twitter.com). Schools most often use a version of the site used by companies where you can control the level of interaction. One of the advantages of these sites is that they are free. At the same time, they can be a challenge to maintain and update.

So, why is it important to have an online presence? Porterfield and Carnes (2010) found several reasons for being online. First, social media helps to build relationships and build support among your stakeholders. Second, parents often come from a different generation than school leaders, one that seeks involvement in school and is comfortable using all forms of social media technology. Third, your families are already commenting about your school online and you want to be part of the conversation. Because a principal has responsibility for maintaining a school's image, social media can be a way to interact with families and community and both share information and listen to their comments.

Blogs—A blog is a website that functions much like a journal or diary. A blog is incredibly flexible and can be used to whatever you want it to be. You can write content, link to other sites or information, and invite people to comment on ideas or respond to an online poll.

Many school leaders use a blog to share their thoughts about their school and its program. It's another way to share information about events, your school's awards and recognitions, good work of students and teachers, and to provide parents with access to resources they can use with their children. There are several sources for creating free online blogs (www.word press.org, www.blogger.com).

Almost every principal we've talked with who has an online presence reports a positive experience. Social media is the fastest growing communication tool in our society, and you'll be well received. Because of its growth among all age groups, social media is not a fad that's going to disappear. While the specific tools may change, social media is here to stay, and there is an increasing expectation that schools, and their leaders, stay connected to both school and community.

Now Try This

_____ Look at and update your school's website and "digital presence"

_____ Examine Facebook and Twitter sites of other schools and see how they use them

_____ Visit the blog of other school leaders to learn how they use social media—http://esheninger.blogspot.com

_____ Check out YouTube (www.youtube.com) as a way to promote your school

Tools to Enhance Productivity

Everyday there are more and more free, online resources that can help school leaders improve productivity. We'll share a few of our favorites, but we know that other tools will be available by the time this book is published.

Coordinating Multiple Calendars—If you use a Smartphone, you probably already use "Cloud" technology to coordinate your calendar across multiple devices. That's essential. For Apple devices, it is iCloud; for Microsoft systems, it's Microsoft Outlook.

Google Calendar (www.google.com/calendar) provides another free online tool to manage your schedule. You'll need a Gmail account (also free) but it is a worthwhile option. Google Calendar allows you to share your schedule, synch functions, and send invitations for meetings and other events. It will also sync with Microsoft Outlook and Apple iCal.

Scheduling Meetings—One of our favorite tools for scheduling meetings is Doodle (www.doodle.com). It's free, easy to use and navigate. To arrange a meeting you identify possible meeting times, send the times to participants asking them to respond, and then confirm a time based on the information you receive from participants.

Doodle has other functions as well. You can use MeetMe so that others can see when you are available to meet, and it allows others to submit meeting requests directly to you. There are other meeting planners that are free or low cost. They include When is Good (http://whenisgood.net) and Google Calendar (described earlier).

Enhancing Collaboration—A wiki is a way to manage complex projects. It's a combination of a website to post material like meeting agendas and minutes, as well as a place where participants can post, revise, and edit work. It allows groups to collaborate on planning and implementing projects and can be an online repository of materials related to a project.

Wikis include discussion forums where participants can communicate about progress on the project and collaborate to prepare materials. Like the other tools in this chapter, there are many sites for free wikis. Our favorite is Wikispaces (www.wikispaces.com) primarily because it provides a free for educators that is ad free and can be made private for additional security.

Recently Ron was working with a suburban Chicago school district to examine their middle grades program and make recommendations for strengthening the program. One of the tools they used was a wiki. Ron and other members posted readings for participants to review and the administration posted data about the school including demographics, achievement data, and the results of a recent climate survey. Members shared their thoughts about the readings and were able to participate in an online discussion about the data. The wiki allowed the group to have a thoughtful discussion prior to the meeting and to the topics to be discussed more fully in a face-to-face meeting.

Shared Documents—Google provides an incredible array of technology tools and almost all of them are free. GoogleDocs (http://docs.google.com) allows users to create word documents, spreadsheets, and presentations, and share them with others. Invitations can be made so that others can edit the docs and collaborate on the final product. Publishing online in GoogleDocs allows you to decide who can look at the material. Your documents can be moved easily into your desktop applications.

Now Try This

_____ Use Doodle (www.doodle.com) to schedule a meeting

_____ Visit Wikispaces (www.wikispaces.com) to learn about how to collaborate online

Tools for Professional Growth

The most successful school leaders recognize the importance of supporting the continued professional growth of their teachers, and for themselves. Traditional forms of professional development were often expensive and required convening large groups of staff for delivery.

More contemporary professional learning models promoted by *Learning Forward* (www.learningforward.org), formerly the National Staff Development Council, focus much more on professional learning onsite with emphasis on learning that improves the learning of all students. Many of those strategies are cost-effective and include forms of virtual learning, access to an array of online materials and resources, and participation in online networks of teachers across multiple sites.

Online Learning—Another of our favorite sites is Moodle (www.moodle. org), a site for managing online courses and virtual learning. Teachers use Moodle to create online discussions for students, and principals use it to promote learning among their teachers. Originally designed for online courses, most people use parts of the site to create forums to discuss school improvement projects. Moodle has become a site for collaborative learning communities. It's free to download and registration is optional.

In *The School Leader's Guide to Social Media* (Williamson & Johnston, 2012) we described several ways Moodle can be used to promote professional learning.

- Create an online workshop
- Organize a discussion group for the School Improvement Team
- Establish a book study group
- Replace announcements at faculty meetings, freeing time for other work
- Arrange a discussion for a curriculum development project.

Another online tool is edWeb.net (www.edWeb.net), a social networking site for people working in the education community. It's a place to share information, learn about best practice, connect with others, and participate in professional development. Just like the other tools, registration is free. Here are examples of how to use edWeb.net for professional learning.

- Organize a discussion group around an issue your school is facing.
- Join the "Lunch and Learn" series to discuss a topic.
- Share ideas with other school leaders.
- Create a discussion about implementing the Common Core standards in your school.

Professional Learning Networks (PLNs)—A PLN is a new term used to describe your network of friends and colleagues who support your learning. While many PLNs are face-to-face, it is possible to expand your network of colleagues using online tools.

These virtual PLNs allow you to share ideas, critique one another's work, access resources, and participate in discussions. Ron uses Twitter for his PLN. He created a Twitter account and then "liked" several professional associations like ASCD (www.ascd.org) and NASSP (www.nassp.org) as well as several known experts in educational leadership. It's amazing to see the resources that arrive every day and the information that he's able to access.

LinkedIn (www.linkedin.com) is a tool to maintain an online resume. We've found that LinkedIn is an accepted and credible way to establish a professional presence online and build a network of professional colleagues and contacts. LinkedIn allows you to stay up-to-date with your professional contacts, exchange information and share ideas, expand your professional affiliations, and enhance your career. LinkedIn membership is free but there are for-fee options to expand your membership.

Like many of the other tools, Google provides a tool for creating a PLN (http://sites.google.com/site/buildidngapln/). Another useful site is Once a Teacher (http://tinyurl.com/olousp). You can use a variety of tools for different networks of colleagues and contacts. Twitter might be for your PLN, Facebook for family and friends, and LinkedIn for professional contacts.

Now Try This

_____ Survey your staff about their social media skills

_____ Model the use of social media for your own professional learning

_____ Subscribe to a school leader's blog (http://connectedprincipals.com)

_____ Have staff showcase social media use during meetings (http://blog.edmondo.com/2012/01/06/edmondo-mini-lesson-showcase)

Final Thoughts

Technology provides school leaders with a whole set of free, or low cost, tools to enhance their operation in an era of declining resources. There are tools to strengthen communication, improve productivity, and promote professional learning. One thing we're sure of is that every year, there will be more and more online tools available to school leaders. It's important that leaders become familiar with the ways that technology can be used to improve their schools and the educational experience of their students.

Resources

School Leaders Need to Harness Technology and Social Media

http://plpnetwork.com/2011/12/20/review-what-connected-school-leaders-do/

This article provides explicit examples of how principals can use technology to enhance teaching and learning in their organization.

Leader Models by Digital Example

www.edweek.org/dd/articles/2013/02/06/02leaders.h06.html

Watch this video from *Education Week* where a school leader discusses how he promotes the use of technology tools by modeling their use and demonstrating how they can improve teaching and learning.

Resources and References

Adams, C. (n.d.) Building business bridges. *Scholastic Administr@tor Magazine*. Retrieved from www.scholastic.com/browse/article.jsp?id=3747462

American School Bus Council. (2013). *Environmental benefits of bus transportation*. Retrieved from www.americanschoolbuscouncil.org/issues/environmental-benefits

Astuto, T. A., Clark, D. L., Read, A., McGree, K. & Fernandez, L. deK. P. (1993). *Challenges to Dominant Assumptions Controlling Educational Reform*. Andover, MA: Regional Laboratory for the Educational Improvement of the Northeast and Islands.

Austin, E. W., Chen, Y., Pinkleton, B. E., & Johnson, J. Q. (March 1, 2006). Benefits and costs of *Channel One* in a middle school setting and the role of media literacy training. *Pediatrics*, 117(3), 423–433. Retrieved from http://pediatrics.aappublications.org/content/117/3/e423.full

Austin ISD. (2013a). *School bus advertising*. Retrieved from www.austinisd.org/transportation/busadvertising

Austin ISD. (2013b). *School bus advertising: frequently asked questions*. Retrieved from www.austinisd.org/transportation/faq

Barnes, F. (April, 2004). *Inquiry and action: Making school improvement part of daily practice*. Providence, RI: Annenberg Institute for School Reform at Brown University. Retrieved from http://annenberginstitute.org/tools/guide/SIGuide_intro.pdf

Barone, L. (2009). *How companies should respond to negative reviews*. Retrieved from http://outspokenmedia.com/reputation-management/respond-negative-reviews/

Barr, M., & McClellan, G. (2011). *Budget and Financial Management in Higher Education.* San Francisco, CA: Jossey-Bass.

Blaydes, J. (2003). *The Educator's Book of Quotes.* Thousand Oaks, CA: Corwin Press.

Bolman, L., & Deal, T. (2008). *Reframing Organizations: Artistry, Choice and Leadership* (4th ed.). San Francisco, CA: Jossey-Bass.

Brame, C. (2013). *Flipping the Classroom.* Nashville, TN: Center for Teaching, Vanderbilt University. Retrieved from http://cft.vanderbilt.edu/teaching-guides/teaching-activities/flipping-the-classroom/

Brenner, J. & Smith, A. (2013). 72% of Online Adults are Social Networking Site Users. Retrieved from www.pewinternet.org/Reports/2013/social-networking-sites.aspx

Business and Education Partnership Advisory Council (BEPAC). (2014). *Frequently Asked Questions.* Cecil County (MD) School District. Elkton, MD: Author.

Cincinnati Youth Collaborative. (2013). *Vision, Mission and History.* Cincinnati, OH: Author. Retrieved from www.cycyouth.org/cyc-pages.php?page_id=1

City, E. (2013). Leadership in challenging times. *Educational Leadership,* 70(7), 10–14.

Council for Corporate and School Partnerships. (n.d.). A *how-to guide for school-business partnerships.* Available from New Hampshire Scholars, Concord, NH. Retrieved from www.nhscholars.org/School-Business%20How_to_Guide1.pdf

Dewey, J. (1902). *The School and Society.* Chicago, IL: University of Chicago Press.

DuFour, R., DuFour, R., Eaker, R. & Many, T. (2010). *Learning by Doing: A Handbook for Professional Learning Communities* (2nd ed.). Bloomington, IN: Solution Tree.

Duncan, A. (November 17, 2010). *The New Normal—Doing More with Less.* Speech to the American Enterprise Institute. Washington, DC: U.S. Department of Education. Retrieved from www.ed.gov/news/speeches/new-normal-doing-more-less-secretary-arne-duncans-remarks-american-enterprise-institut

Edison, T.A. (n.d.). Thomas A. Edison Quotes. BrainyQuote. Retrieved from www.brainyquote.com/quotes/authors/t/thomas_a_edison.html

Emanuel, R. (2008, November 19). Interview. Wall Street Journal CEO Council, Washington, DC. Retrieved from www.youtube.com/watch?v=_mzcbXi1Tkk

Fletcher, A. (2002). Fist-to-five consensus-building. *Freechild Project.* Retrieved from www.freechild.org/Firestarter/Fist2Five.htm

Foundation Center. (2013a). *The Foundation Directory.* Washington, DC: Author. Retrieved from: http://fconline.foundationcenter.org/

Foundation Center. (2013b). *Knowledge Base: How Do I Write a Grant Proposal?* Washington, DC: Author. Retrieved from http://grantspace.org/Tools/Knowledge-Base/Funding-Research/Proposal-Writing/grant-proposals

Fountain Valley Education Foundation. (2013). *Our Students. Our Community. Our Concern.* Fountain Valley, CA: Author. Retrieved from http://fvef.org/

Frank, W. (2005). *These 10 core competencies comprise good leadership.* Retrieved from the *Denver Business Journal,* www.bizjournals.com/denver/stories/2005/08/29/smallb3.html

Fullan, M. (2001). *Leading in a Culture of Change.* San Francisco, CA: Jossey-Bass.

Garmston, R. & Wellman, B. (1999). *The adaptive school: A sourcebook for developing collaborative groups.* Norwood, MA: Christopher-Gordon.

Henderson, A., Mapp, K., Johnson, V., & Davies, D. (2007). *Beyond the Bake Sale.* New York: The New Press.

Hord, S., Rutherford, W., Huling-Austin, L., & Hall, G. (1987). *Taking Charge of Change.* Alexandria, VA: Association for Supervision and Curriculum Development.

Hoy, W. K. & Tarter, J. (2008). *Administrators Solving the Problems of Practice: Decision-Making Concepts, Cases and Consequences* (3rd ed.). Boston: Pearson Education.

Irving, W. (1824). *Tales of a Traveler.* New York: American Publishers.

Johnston, J. H. (2009, October). Dancing partners: schools and businesses. *The School Administrator,* 9(66), 24–28. Retrieved from www.aasa.org/SchoolAdministratorArticle.aspx?id=6936

Johnston, J. H. (2011). *Securing volunteers to fix up the school.* Research Brief prepared for Education Partnerships, Inc. Retrieved from www.educationpartnerships.org

Johnston, J. H. (March, 2013). Return on investment (ROI) for local philanthropy. Chart Lines occasional paper, St. Petersburg, FL. Chart 411.

Knapp, M., Copland, M. & Talbert, J. (2003). *Leading for Learning: Reflective Tools for School and District Leaders.* Seattle, WA: Center for the Study of Teaching and Policy.

Lenhart, A., Purcell, K., Smith, A. & Zickuhr, K. (2010). Social media and young adults. A report from the Pew Internet and American Life Project. Retrieved from www.pewinternet.org/Reports/2010/Social-Media-and-Young-Adults.aspx

Levenson, N. (2012). *Smarter Budgets, Smarter Schools: How to Survive and Thrive in Tight Times.* Cambridge, MA: Harvard Education Press. Retrieved from www.hepg.org/hep/book/163/SmarterBudgetsSmarterSchools

Levenson, N. (2012, December). *Strategies for Smarter Budgets, Smarter Schools.* Policy Brief. Dayton, OH: Thomas B. Fordham Institute.

McCabe, C. (November, 2007). Writing grants. *NEA Today.* Retrieved from www.nea.org/home/10476.htm

Maddox, D. C. (1999). *Budgeting for Non-Profit Organizations.* New York: Wiley.

Mangleburg, T. F. (1990). Children's influence in purchase decisions: A review and critique. In Goldberg, M. E., Gorn, G., & Pollay, R. W. (Eds.), *Advances in Consumer Research,* Volume 17 (pp. 813–825). Provo, UT: Association for Consumer Research.

Mann, H. (1872). Thoughts on education. In Mann, M., *Thoughts Selected from the Writings of Horace Mann.* Boston: Lee and Shepherd Publishers.

Marzano, R., Waters, T. & McNulty, B. (2005). *School Leadership that Works: From Research to Results.* Alexandria, VA: Association for Supervision and Curriculum Development.

Miami-Dade County Schools. (2013, September). *School Based Advertising Guide, Division of Athletics, Activities and Accreditation.* Policy Manual., Miami-Dade County Public Schools. Miami, FL: Author. Retrieved from http://ehandbooks.dadeschools.net/policies/12.pdf

National Conference of State Legislatures (2010). Four day school weeks. Retrieved from www.ncsl.org/research/education/school-calendar-four-day-school-week-overview.aspx

National School Public Relations Association. (2010). *Dealing with rumors spawned by text messages.* Retrieved from http://nspra.org/node/3072

Noguchi, S. (2013, March 2). California's ban on school fees causes confusion. *San Jose Mercury News.* Retrieved from www.mercurynews.com/ci_22702203/new-california-school-law-that-bans-fees-causes

Petrilli, M. (2012, April). *How Districts can Stretch the School Dollar.* Policy Brief. Dayton, OH: Thomas B. Fordham Institute.

Petrilli, M. J., & M. Roza (2011, January). *Stretching the School Dollar: A Brief for State Policy-makers.* Policy Brief. Dayton, OH: Thomas B. Fordham Institute.

Porterfield, K., & Carnes, M. (2010). *10 reasons you should pay attention to social media.* Retrieved from http://aasa.org/TenSocialMediaTips.aspx?terms=social+media

Protheroe, N. (2011). Effective resource use—People, time, money. *Principal's Research Review,* 6(3), 1–6.

Public Impact for The Chicago Public Education Fund. (2008). *School Turnaround Leaders: Competencies for Success.* Chapel Hill, NC: Public Impact.

Rampell, C. (2011, April 15). On school buses, ad space for rent. *New York Times.* Retrieved from www.nytimes.com/2011/04/16/business/media/16buses.html?_r=0

Roseville Area Schools. (2008). *Policy 700—Advertising.* Retrieved from www.isd623.org/schoolboard/documents/623Policies/700PAdvertising.pdf

Ryman, A. (2004, January 4). Schools get big bucks in soda deals. *Arizona Republic.* Tempe, AZ: Education Policy Studies Laboratory. Retrieved from www.asu.edu/educ/epsl/CERU/Articles/CERU-0401–188-OWI.doc

Shapiro, J., & Stefkovich, J. (2011). *Ethical Leadership and Decision-making in Education* (3rd ed.). New York: Routledge.

Shell US (2014). *Request for a Grant from Shell US: FAQs.* Retrieved from www.shell.us/environment-society/grant.html

Simon, S. (May 25, 2011). Public schools charge kids for basics, frills. *The Wall Street Journal*. Retrieved from http://online.wsj.com/news/articles/SB10001424052748703864204576313572363698678

Spence, L., & Spence, S. (1993). *Competence at Work*. New York: John Wiley.

Statistic Brain. (n.d.) *Teenage consumer spending statistics*. Retrieved from www.statisticbrain.com/teenage-consumer-spending-statistics/

Steep Creek Media. (2013). Introducing a unique advertising opportunity. Retrieved from http://steepcreekmedia.com/

Story, L. (2007, January 15). Anywhere the eye can see it's likely to see an ad. *New York Times*. Retrieved from www.nytimes.com/2007/01/15/business/media/15everywhere.html?pagewanted=all&_r=0

Tennessee State Board of Education (2009, January 30). *School Fees, Rule*. Nashville, TN: Author. Retrieved from www.state.tn.us/sbe/2009Januarypdfs/IV%20A%20School%20Fees%20Rule.pdf

Turner, D. (2011, November 19). Georgia school district looks at ads to make money. *AJC.COM, The Atlanta Journal and Constitution*. Retrieved from www.ajc.com/news/news/local/ga-school-district-looks-at-ads-to-make-money-1/nQNqj/

University of Wisconsin—Milwaukee. (2013). *Hybrid Courses*. Milwaukee, WI: Author. Retrieved from www4.uwm.edu/ltc/hybrid/index.cfm

Valenti, R. (2009, January). Expanding the fiscal toolbox. *The School Administrator*, (1), 66.

Walberg, H. J. (2011). *Achieving More, Spending Less in Schools, Districts, and States*. Lincoln, IL: Center on Innovation & Improvement. Retrieved from www.centerii.org/productivity/docs/achieving_more_spending_less2.pdf

Walter, K. (2004). *Making Good Choices: Sustainable School Improvement*. Naperville, IL: Learning Point Associates.

Westmoreland, H., Rosenberg, H., Lopez, M. E., & Weiss, H. (2009). *Seeing Is Believing: Promising Practices for How School Districts Promote Family Engagement*. Cambridge, MA: Harvard Family Project.

Whitehurst, G. J., & Chingos, M. M. (2011). *Class Size: What Research Says and What It Means for State Policy*. Washington, DC: Brown Center on Education Policy at Brookings. Retrieved from www.brookings.edu/research/papers/2011/05/11-class-size-whitehurst-chingos

Williamson, R. (1998). *Scheduling Schools: Tools for Improved Student Achievement*. Reston, VA: National Association of Secondary School Principals.

Williamson, R. (2008, March). *The schedule as a tool to improve student learning*. NASSP Middle Level Leader e-Newsletter. Retrieved from www.nassp.org/Content.aspx?topic=57198

Williamson, R. (2009). *Scheduling to Improve Student Learning*. Westerville, OH: National Middle School Association.

Williamson, R. (2010). *Economy's Impact on Schools*. Research Brief prepared for Education Partnerships, Inc. Retrieved from http://gearup.ous.edu/sites/default/files/Research-Briefs/ResearchBriefEconomyImpactonSchools.pdf

Williamson, R. D. (April, 2011). *Dealing with Budget Cuts*. Research Brief prepared for Education Partnerships, Inc. Retrieved http://gearup.ous.edu/sites/default/files/Research-Briefs/ResearchBriefBudgetReductions.pdf

Williamson, R., & Blackburn, B. (2009). *The Principalship from A to Z*. Larchmont, NY: Eye on Education.

Williamson, R., & Blackburn, B. (2010). *Rigorous Schools and Classrooms: Leading the Way*. Larchmont, NY: Eye on Education.

Williamson, R., & Blackburn, B. (2011). *Rigor in Your School: A Toolkit for Leaders*. Larchmont, NY: Eye on Education.

Williamson, R., & Johnston, J. H. (2012). *The School Leader's Guide to Social Media*. Larchmont, NY: Eye on Education.